CW00850693

To Steve, My Prince Charming

You opened my eyes to the possibilities of love.....

My petals are starting to unfurl..

from your little Sunflower

Francesca Ross

1st copy off the press!

Arabella's Journey

Francesca Ross

authorHOUSE®

AuthorHouse™ UK Ltd.
500 Avebury Boulevard
Central Milton Keynes, MK9 2BE
www.authorhouse.co.uk
Phone: 08001974150

First published by AuthorHouse 11/17/2009

ISBN: 978-1-4490-4167-0 (sc)

Foreword

Married to a rich and successful financial banker, Sebastian, and the mother of a young daughter, Chloe, Arabella had everything and spent her days shopping or 'doing lunch' with her friends. All was great in her life until the fateful day she realises that her husband is having an affair. Embarking on a journey of self discovery, Arabella travels to America to visit Charlotte, a friend she's known since her schooldays. On the flight to America, she meets a man called Jensen. Unbeknown to Arabella, Jensen was about to turn her life upside down! Discovering who the other woman is, in Sebastian's life, Arabella is shocked to the core. Extending her stay in America to allow herself more time to come to terms with her situation, Arabella is unsure what to do about her husband's affair. Does she turn a blind eye, confront him and try to make their marriage work, or leave him.

On marrying Sebastian, Arabella had given up her career to become a full- time wife and mother, running after Sebastian, organising the dinner parties he would arrange to impress his business contacts. Following a telephone call from her parents, Arabella is forced to return to England when her daughter has a serious accident, an accident which leaves Arabella with a very difficult decision to make. Arabella starts to see those around her in their true colours as she leads her rollercoaster life. Would Jensen be the man to save her?

Join Arabella in this heart wrenching story. Experience the emotion, the grief and the pain, as well as the good times, laughter, and the hope that she finds. Enjoy too, the romance, love, sex, and lust as Arabella embarks on her new life! As you read each page, you'll find yourself going through all of Arabella's emotions. You won't be disappointed!

CHAPTER 1

Let me introduce myself, my name is Arabella, and some people say that I have it all, a rich and attentive husband, and an adorable four year old daughter, Chloe. My days are filled with a combination of expensive shopping trips, or 'doing lunch' with the girls. I can't deny that life has been good to me, I wear expensive clothes, eat in the best restaurants, and have my own bank account with a six figure sum in it, courtesy of my husband Sebastian. When we were first married I thought Sebastian was being generous with his money because he didn't want me to go short of anything, but these days, I get the distinct feeling that the money is always readily available so I can keep myself busy and out of his way, so I don't bother him. I know that I have more than most, but I can't help feeling that something is missing, but I don't know what! For the last few years I'd almost been on autopilot, saying the right things at the right time, and making the right gestures when expected of me. I couldn't blame my husband, Sebastian, for the way I was feeling, he was loving, kind and thoughtful when we were together, a good provider and a good father to our daughter, Chloe, so why did I feel so empty inside?

Today seemed just like any other day, our nanny had taken Chloe to the park, as normal, which meant that I had time on my hands and could hit the shops for a spot of retail therapy. Today however, I'd decided to stay at home and do something different. I went downstairs to talk to Sebastian, to see if I could tempt him to play hooky from work so we could spend the day together, maybe grab a bite of lunch at our favourite pub by the canal, or even just spend the day cuddling up together in bed. It had been such a long time since we'd done that, in fact it had been a long time since we'd done much of anything together. I suppose life had just got in the way. I was too busy being a perfect wife and doting mother, while Sebastian was working all the hours God sent! As I approached Sebastian's study I heard him talking on the telephone. I paused awhile, not daring to enter, as Sebastian didn't like to be disturbed when he was working in his study. It was a sort of unwritten rule that, when he was working I wasn't to disturb him. As I carried on listening, to see if I could make out when it would be appropriate to go in and talk to him I overheard his conversation, and the words began to swim around in my head. I felt faint and dizzy, did I really hear Sebastian, My Sebastian, tell someone that he loved and missed them and was counting the hours until they met that evening? Oh my God! I couldn't believe it, Sebastian was having an affair!

I heard the click of the receiver, as Sebastian put the telephone down, so I quickly turned towards the stairs. As I did so, Sebastian called out to me. What was I going to say? How was I supposed to react? All I kept thinking was, that if I didn't sit down my legs were going to give way. I couldn't make out what Sebastian was saying to me when he caught up with me on the stairs, his words had cut like a knife, I couldn't breathe and I felt sick. All of a sudden everything went black, and the next thing I knew, I was coming round and looking up to Sebastian's concerned face. How could he do this to me? I was a good wife and a good mother, was everything in our life together a lie? Sebastian told me he was going to call a doctor but I wouldn't let him. I wanted to shout at him, and tell him that a doctor couldn't cure what I was suffering from! I felt shattered and broken, that the man I loved could do such a thing to me, but as I opened my mouth, words failed me. All I could manage was a pathetic squeak! Sebastian suggested that I must be pining for something. 'Pining for something?' I thought. 'I was! My husband! The one I married, the loving, caring, man he once was, not the lying, cheating, bastard he had become!' I wanted to spill the beans and tell him what I had heard. I wanted to see his reaction. Make him explain, and beg my forgiveness, but all I could do was manage to mumble that I was alright. I stood up and stumbled upstairs. Sebastian didn't even follow me! Instead he just shouted up that he was working late, and not to wait up for him!

I spent the rest of the day in bed, thinking about all the times he had told me he was working late. Had he been seeing her? Who was she? Did she even know that he was married, and had a daughter? My mind was racing! I was consumed with rage and wanted to kill him! Then my anger turned to self-pity and I couldn't stop crying helplessly. What was I going to do? I knew I couldn't make any rash decisions, after all I had Chloe to consider! I needed to talk to someone, someone who would listen to me and give me an honest opinion, so I decided to ring my best friend, Charlotte. I had known Charlotte since we were at school. We were inseparable, and even when I started going out with Sebastian, our friendship didn't suffer, as so many other friendships do, in fact, we had become an inseparable trio. Sebastian had warmed to Charlotte straight away, and for many years we spent a lot of time in each other's company. When Charlotte had man trouble she would ask Sebastian for advice from a male perspective. Then a year ago, out of the blue, Charlotte suddenly announced that she was moving to America, that she'd been offered a promotion at work and would be leaving within a week. I kept ringing Charlotte's mobile number but couldn't get any answer.

Suddenly, I was aware of Chloe's voice. She and our nanny had returned from the park, I knew that I had to keep things 'normal' for Chloe's sake, so I decided to carry on as if everything was fine. For the next few days

I went onto auto-pilot just to get me through the days. I needed to give myself time to think things through. I didn't want to live a lie, but I didn't want to lose Sebastian either! The one thing I knew for certain was that I couldn't share him! I decided to ask my parents to look after Chloe so that I could go and visit Charlotte in America. I had been meaning to go and see her, but every time I spoke to Sebastian about it he said that he couldn't get the time off work, and he would never consider letting me go on my own. But, after everything that had happened recently, I knew that, with or without Sebastian's blessing, I needed to go!

I called the airport and booked my ticket, and arranged with my parents to collect Chloe from our nanny, later in the afternoon. Everything was set for my trip to America. The only problem I had was that I still couldn't contact Charlotte. I was wondering what to do, whether I should just get on the plane and take a chance on eventually getting in touch with Charlotte, or wait and see if she contacted me, following all the answer-phone messages that I'd left her. I just knew, if only for my own sanity, I needed to get away. I tried contacting Charlotte once more, but still couldn't get through, so I left another message saying that I was coming to see her. I contemplated what I was going to tell Sebastian. I knew I didn't owe him an explanation and, in fact, I decided I wasn't going to tell Sebastian anything! I wasn't even going to leave him a note! I knew that Sebastian would be worried. On reflection, I realised that he always knew where I was, you could even say I was very predictable. No wonder he found it easy to have an affair! 'It might do him some good to wonder where I was, not to have that control, wondering when I would be home, or if I was coming home at all!' I thought. I was going to let him feel for a change, what It felt like, waiting for him to come home, or wondering if he was going to stay in our city apartment because he didn't want to disturb me by coming home late. What a fool I'd been, trusting everything he said, and believing all his lies. Maybe I knew, deep down, that things were not right between us. Perhaps that's why I felt so empty inside, unfulfilled, and lonely.

One thing I knew for certain was that I couldn't go back to being good old reliable Arabella. I needed to change, I wanted to change. Sebastian's affair had left me feeling very vulnerable. It was a feeling I didn't much care for! I had always been so confident and outgoing, so sure of myself, but this had took the wind out of my sails! It left me with a feeling of not knowing what to do, or what I wanted any more. My confidence had gone and my ego was bruised, how was I going to get through it?

My taxi arrived to take me to the airport. I picked up my suitcase, and strolled through the front door, locking it behind me. Walking down the path, I turned back to look up at my house, the place I used to call my home. It certainly didn't feel like home and I wondered if it ever could be again. This house used to be my retreat. Was that gone forever? I turned and headed for the taxi, not daring to give my home a second look. I could feel the tears welling in my eyes, but I had to be strong. I couldn't afford to give in to my feelings, as it would leave me an emotional wreck. Nothing had fazed me before. I was the backbone of my family! When things were not going to plan, everyone relied on me to see things through, to give encouragement and guidance, that problems could be overcome. That was my role in life, to keep things running smoothly. The taxi ride to the airport seemed to take forever. We seemed to stop at every set of traffic lights, and at one point I didn't think I was going to get there and make my flight. It felt like everything was against me getting away to sort my life out. The queue for the check-in desk was about a mile long, and everybody seemed to have excess baggage. People around me were frantically trying to distribute the contents of their cases equally, so that their luggage could be accepted on the flight. I began to scan the airport. I was always a bit of a people watcher. I studied the people around me, and saw so many different types of people. There was the business executive, who travelled the world living out of a suitcase, and who would probably have a heart attack by the age of Fifty through the stress of chasing just one more deal. Then there was Mr & Mrs Two-point-four kids, with their matching sweaters and matching luggage. Then my eyes caught sight of 'The Honeymooners' Their eyes gazing at each other with such love and hope, boy were they in for a shock! 'God!' I thought, 'I was turning cynical!' But I couldn't help looking over at The Honeymooners, the way he held his wife so protectively, and the way his wife responded by putting her arms around him and holding on so tight. I wondered if I would ever feel like that again.

At long last, I was on the plane, so I settled down in my seat for the long flight ahead. A blonde haired gentleman had sat down beside me. He had a rather boyish smile, and wore scruffy denim jeans and jacket. He was attractive in a rugged sort of way, not my usual suited type, but nevertheless, appealing. I was shocked at how condescending and judgemental I had become over the years. I never dreamt of becoming such a snob, like the rest of my friends, and although I hated to admit it, that's just what I'd become. The gentleman introduced himself as Jensen. He said that he was going to New England to start a new life, after being dumped at the altar for his best man! 'How ironic,' I thought 'Was everyone on this plane running away from someone or something, to start afresh. The more Jensen and I talked, the more I was feeling settled in his company. He seemed genuinely nice and the more I listened to his words the more I was becoming attracted to his boyish smile. 'Pull yourself together,' I thought to myself 'You're supposed to be mourning for the lost trust, and deception that your husband's inflicted on you, not behaving like a love-struck teenager.' But I couldn't help it, Jensen made me feel at ease. I didn't need to pretend to be something I wasn't, I could be myself, but who was I? Did I truly know who I was, or for so long, had I just been the person Sebastian wanted me to be? This was going to be a journey that was fated to happen. I was going to learn so much more than I had first realised. Not only was I exploring my future with Sebastian, but I was going to find out who I was, I wasn't sure if I would be able to cope! As the plane made its way across the skies, I had found common ground with Jensen and our laughter filled the aeroplane. Did I say laughter? I felt like I'd known Jensen for years, and I began to feel comfortable in his presence, comfortable enough to pour my heart out to him about why I was going to see my friend, Charlotte.

He said that he couldn't understand why someone could do such a thing. I'd have to agree with him on that! Jensen said that I seemed so kind, caring, and thoughtful..........and beautiful! I hadn't thought of myself as beautiful before. I always tried to make an effort with my appearance, but my figure had taken a battering after the birth of Chloe. Everything had gone South, the only upside to having droopy boobs, that I could see, was that whenever it was cold, I didn't need to wear a thermal vest to keep my stomach warm, as my boobs sat there!

Sebastian had often remarked how I had changed since Chloe was born. I thought that he was commenting on my mothering skills, obviously not. It was probably more correct that he was commenting on my not so firm body. Maybe it was the way I looked, maybe Sebastian didn't find me attractive anymore. You read about these women in Cosmopolitan magazine, things like that happened to them, not me! Maybe that was why he had an affair! If I think back, the danger signs had been there all along. Sebastian had thought that I had let myself go, how could I have been so blind? It was all my fault, that's why he had an affair, I drove him to it. I had to admit, I had spent a lot of time on Chloe. She needed me because she was so young, and I suppose that I had put Sebastian second, but it hadn't been my intention, it was just that Chloe had needed me more. I knew that Sebastian felt second best, but that wasn't true. I loved him with all my heart and soul, it's just that when you become a mum for the first time it's not easy, your hormones are all over the place, and you wonder if you're doing things right. When you give birth, no-one gives you a manual to tell you what to do, you just learn as you go along. I didn't mean to shut Sebastian out, I just thought he'd realise that taking care of our daughter would take priority for a while. 'It must have been my fault,' I thought again, 'I drove him to it, or did I?' I was beginning to wonder. The way Jensen was talking to me and listening to me, made me think that Sebastian had an affair because of his own ego, his own selfish way. For the first time in my life, maybe, just maybe, I wasn't to blame. Perhaps this was a situation that I couldn't prevent or make better.

It turned out that Jensen was staying in the same town as me, and he wanted to meet up with me again. He suggested we could go for a drink or maybe a meal. Jensen filled me with excitement, I couldn't walk away from him now, not after he had made such an impact on me, I didn't know what was going to happen between us, if anything. All I knew was that I wanted to see him again soon, very soon. Jensen had ignited something that I hadn't felt for such a long time, and I wanted to explore this feeling more. In fact, I needed to explore why a stranger had made me feel this way, a feeling that had been so deeply buried for such a long time, that I'd forgotten what it felt like.

Jensen had started to fall asleep next to me and his head was leant against my shoulder, and partly on my chest. I could feel my body start to tingle with desire as he rested against me. I could smell the scent of his aftershave, I knew this smell, as it happened to be my favourite aftershave but somehow, it smelled nicer on Jensen than I had remembered it. I wanted him, I needed him. I wanted Jensen to take me in his arms, and feel his body next to mine. I wanted him to kiss my aching lips, they were aching with such passion that I felt on fire, and nothing could put out the flames of passion. I was aware that my breathing had become heavy and this made me feel like my head was swaying. I felt tipsy with emotion, and my lips were dry and aching. I longed for Jensen to touch me and make me feel alive again. My eyes skimmed Jensen's body, he had a great physique. He had broad, tanned, shoulders and strong arms, arms I was sure would make me feel safe if they were around me. Jensen moved slightly and his head fell further onto my chest. His body scent smelled heavenly and made me want to explode! I could feel my nipples standing erect, pushing hard against my blouse in anticipation of it all, my body was on fire and I just needed a release. It was probably better that Jensen was asleep, and unaware of the raging passion that he'd ignited inside me. I hadn't felt this for such a long time, and I wasn't sure if I could handle the way I was feeling! Maybe Jensen wouldn't be able to handle it either!

I was suddenly brought out of my daydream by the captain announcing that we were about to land, and had to fasten our safety belts. I gently roused Jensen from his slumber, and said that he had better get himself ready. He smiled at me and gave me a wink, blissfully unaware of the torrent of emotion that he had stirred up inside of me. On landing, we exchanged mobile telephone numbers and Jensen promised to be in touch. He said that he hoped that I would see him again, and not forget him! One thing was certain, Jensen wouldn't be forgotten, especially as he had made me feel alive again. 'Oh yes, I was definitely going to see him again!'

The airport was full of hustle and bustle, and the whole world and his wife were waiting for their luggage. I was tired and I just wanted to get my suitcase and find the nearest telephone, so I could ring Charlotte and tell her that I had finally arrived, seeing as my mobile needed charging. After what seemed like an hour, I had retrieved my suitcase and made my way to the airport telephones. There was still no reply from Charlotte's. I wondered if she had gone away on holiday. I began to feel that I had made a terrible mistake, I was stuck in a country that I didn't know and I started to think that this wasn't one of the brightest ideas I'd had. Maybe I'd bitten off more than I could chew. Perhaps I shouldn't have embarked on my journey until I'd been in touch with Charlotte, and made sure that it would okay to stay with her. I decided that the best thing to do would be to find a hotel and get some sleep, as the jetlag was starting to kick in, and after a good night's sleep I could then ring Charlotte and sort things out.

I found a hotel in Vermont. It wasn't far from where Charlotte lived. As soon as I got to my hotel room I headed for a long soak in the Jacuzzi. It was just what I needed. After what seemed like an hour, I emerged, relaxed and in need of some sustenance. I scanned the hotel's room service menu and decided on a chicken sandwich, with a glass of Perrier water. After I had eaten I settled down for the night in my queen size bed, and gently drifted off to sleep.

The next morning I awoke to the Sun gleaming through the window. 'What a beautiful day.' I thought as I got myself dressed and went down to breakfast. I feasted on home-made muffins, and pancakes drizzled with Maple syrup, and a whole pot of strong, black coffee. I finished breakfast and made my way up to my room to call Chloe and see how she was. She was playing in the garden with her cousins and she sounded like she was having a great time, as I could hear her giggling in the background as I spoke to my mother. I asked if Sebastian had been in touch but he hadn't. So much for missing me, he probably hadn't even noticed that I had gone! 'What could he be thinking? Did he not wonder where his daughter was? Maybe he was too busy with his mistress, and hadn't even gone home yet! God! That man made my blood boil.' I thought to myself. I began to see Sebastian in a different light. He was a very selfish, vain man, and vain was right! He was always preening himself in the mirror, his clothes had to be of a certain make, and his shoes highly polished. A chore which I had spent numerous hours on, I might add! I was expected to be the perfect little hostess when we entertained his business associates on an evening, even though I'd have spent all day cooking, as he refused to employ out-side caterers. Everything had to be perfect, the perfect wife, the perfect family, the biggest house. Everything he had was on show to the whole world. It was as if people judged him through his achievements!

Looking back, everything I did for him, he would criticise. He would often point out how one of his colleagues wives had given such a remarkable dinner party and that, perhaps I should ring her and get a few tips! I suppose I hadn't noticed before, just how demeaning he had become towards me. I just took it for granted that he would say those things to me, not because he was being critical, but because he wanted me to be the best I could be. I wondered how many years I'd spent trying to gain his approval, his love, and maybe, his acceptance. He didn't need the trophy wife that, although I hate to admit it, I'd become, but a slave, someone to carry out his orders to the letter. I couldn't think of one time that I'd questioned his word. I always took it for granted that, when Sebastian made a decision, it was because it was best for us as a family. I suppose, in a twisted kind of way, my finding out about his affair had made me sit up and smell the coffee, and made me think about what I've had to put up with, and the type of person I had become.

When I was younger I was always questioning authority, no one could ever have accused me of being a walkover. I would stand up for what I truly believed in, and made sure everyone knew about it! 'Where was the old me?' I wondered. One thing I knew for sure was that I was going to rediscover the 'younger me', and not let myself be taken for a fool anymore. After all the events of the past few days, I had become stronger, and more aware of how unhappy I had been in my marriage. My first thought, on learning about Sebastian's affair was that I wasn't prepared to share him, but as I sit here now, I'm not sure if I want him at all! I deserved to be treated with respect and that's something Sebastian hadn't done. I'd asked my mum not to tell Sebastian where I'd gone. I wanted to make him suffer, but as usual, her response was for her to ask me what I'd done to upset him, as he would have surely been in touch. You could always count on my mother to support Sebastian's side, indeed, she was amazed when Sebastian asked me to marry him. I think her comment was something like 'Sebastian could have anyone, so why ask you?' As you can see, my mother has always been very supportive......NOT! That's probably why she got on with Sebastian so well, as he used to treat me like she did, with very little respect. Well, all I can say is 'Watch out world, Arabella's back!' I tried Charlotte's number one last time, again there was no reply, I wondered if Sebastian had rung her, and she was avoiding me because she didn't want to get involved. I decided to make my way over to Charlotte's house to see if she was in, but avoiding me. After all I'd flown 'half way round the world' to see her, so I had to, at least try to see her.

I put on my jacket and made my way outside. It was such a beautiful day that I decided to take a slow walk to Charlotte's house. I loved Vermont, it was full of character with beautiful village greens, white-washed churches, and covered bridges, kind of quaint! 'Yes!' I thought 'What a wonderful place to live, so peaceful and tranquil.' I had read somewhere that Vermont was famous for The Green Mountains, in fact, that was where Vermont got its name from. I arrived in Burlington, where Charlotte lived. It was exactly as I'd imagined it, after my many conversations with Charlotte on the telephone. Burlington had a university, and was situated on the shores of Lake Champlain. Most of the hotels were created on a grand scale, and the hotel in which I was staying was no exception. It was called 'The Lake Inn'. It was a very Colonial style building, set in eighteen acres of woodland, with views of the northern peaks of the Green Mountains.

I arrived at Charlotte's house and noticed that her door was open, so I knocked, but there was no reply. I walked inside to see where she was, and heard her on the telephone to someone. Charlotte sounded annoyed, and she shouted down the phone to the person on the other end 'To make a decision, as she couldn't hang around forever!' It sounded like Charlotte too, was having complications in her love life. As Charlotte put down the phone, she turned and saw me standing there. She jumped a little, and asked how long I'd been standing there. I explained that I'd knocked, but didn't get any answer, so I walked in. She looked a bit flustered and asked when I had arrived in Burlington. I told her the whole story about Sebastian, and how I had decided to come and visit her so I could sort out what I was going to do with my life. I missed out the part about Jensen!

'Ah, yes! Jensen.' I hadn't thought about him since yesterday. Charlotte seemed a bit surprised at my visit so I didn't want to shock her any more. My story about Jensen could wait until another day, as I was keen to know why she hadn't replied to any of my phone calls. She explained that she had just returned from a business trip and had, literally, just got in the door when I had arrived. I asked her where she had been, and was surprised to hear that she had, in fact, been in England. I asked her why she hadn't phoned, as we could have met up, but she explained that it had just been a quick visit and she hadn't had time. I thought it odd that she hadn't even rung, but didn't pursue it as she seemed unwilling to talk about it. 'Maybe she'd had a row with the mystery man who was on the phone, while she was over there! Never mind, there would be plenty of time to catch up.' I thought, as I'd planned on staying for at least another week. Charlotte explained that she had some things to attend to over the next couple of days, so she wasn't able to see me until then. She'd work commitments to take care of, so, after a cup of tea, I made my way back to my hotel.

Once back in my room, I wondered what I could do to occupy my time until I was to meet with Charlotte. I noticed a brochure on the coffee table in my room. It was advertising various different activities that were on offer. I decided that I might as well sign up for quite a few of the activities the hotel was offering, as I had nothing else to do. 'If I was going to get to know the place, I might as well start as I mean to go on, and if I happen to enjoy myself, all the better!' I thought. I had a busy schedule ahead, cycling, hiking, and tennis. If anything, I was going to get fit with all that exercise! With the gentle heat of the day, I decided to relax on my hotel bed.

CHAPTER 2

As I lay on my bed pondering what my future held my thoughts drifted back to the previous day, and my meeting with Jensen. I just couldn't get him out of my mind. I still couldn't get my head round the fact that he had made such an impact on me, especially in such a short space of time. Maybe I was susceptible to a bit of attention, seeing as it seemed so long ago since Sebastian and I had shared something so intense. I knew, when I made the decision to get away and put things into perspective, that it would be an 'eye opener', but I didn't bank on it being so daunting and yet so invigorating at the same time. All I knew was that any decision I had to make just couldn't be rushed, I had to be unselfish, and consider Chloe. After all, I didn't want to uproot and unsettle her. I know kids are somewhat resilient and will bounce back, but I still felt uneasy about making any drastic decisions. Meeting Jensen had, I suppose, put another hurdle in my path. I didn't really know if we would ever meet again, but even if we didn't, meeting him had still changed my life! It opened up the possibility of me meeting someone in the future who could treat me with respect, an equal, someone who could unlock the passion in me like Jensen had done.

Sebastian and I didn't really have a good sex life. It wasn't ever 'Earth moving', but nevertheless I didn't complain. I knew we weren't compatible in the bedroom department, maybe I just wasn't enough for Sebastian! Perhaps I didn't do it for him, maybe, just maybe, he didn't do it for me! He certainly didn't make me feel desirable and sexy, or hungry for his touch, like Jensen had. I wondered whether I had the courage to ring Jensen and invite him for dinner. Oh! What was I to do? My heart was telling me to ring him but my head was telling me that I didn't want any more complications in my life at this moment in time. That, I had to admit was true, but I still couldn't stop thinking about him. I felt like a teenager who had a big crush on someone, waiting around just in the hope of seeing him again! I got up and made my way downstairs to take a bit of lunch. The lounge was very cosy. I decided to go and sit by the window overlooking the beautiful lawned gardens. I scanned the lunch menu and settled on poached salmon with new potatoes, and a pot of tea. It was delicious, I felt like a V.I.P. The service was impeccable, with attentive staff and the best china and silverware. It was nice just to sit back and enjoy the peace and quiet, and not constantly worrying about making sure Sebastian had everything he wanted. 'Yes, I could get quite used to feeling like this.' I thought.

After lunch, I took a stroll in the gardens, The air was heavy with scented flowers, I could hear the birds chirping happily away, and a sense of calm filled the air. For the first time in my life I had been selfish, selfish enough to spend this time away from home, and although I felt guilty about leaving Chloe with my parents back home, I knew that she would be enjoying herself. My parents doted on Chloe, and although I wasn't close to them, I couldn't fault their relationship with her. Chloe always followed her grandad around, she was his shadow, and if I'm being honest, my dad loved the attention. He enjoyed pottering around in the garden with her, showing her all the various flowers and plants. Only last week they had finished planting a vegetable plot. Chloe was so proud when she came home, excitedly talking about how she had to dig holes in the ground, plant the seeds and water them. Chloe loved getting caked in mud. I could never dress her in what I'd call pretty clothes, as she always ended up covered in muck from head to toe! Chloe always hated getting dressed up when we had Sebastian's business colleagues over for dinner, as he always insisted that she dressed all girly, with pigtails in her hair. I've got to admit it though, she did look really cute! Chloe felt more at home in her jeans and tee-shirt, she certainly was a tomboy!

Having Chloe had really changed my life. I think I was born to be a mother. Some people take to motherhood straight away, as I did, and some don't. Take for instance, my friend Sarah. She hated it. Maybe hate was too strong a word, but Sarah saw having a family as an added burden. When her daughter Caitlin was born, she put her name down on the 'First Steps' nursery's list straight away. I mean don't get me wrong, First Steps nursery was very exclusive. They teach toddlers etiquette and languages, but I think, although it's good to make sure that your children receive the best education possible, I still think kids should be allowed and encouraged to have fun and play, kids grow up far too quickly these days! My one regret concerning Chloe, was that I let Sebastian bully me into hiring a nanny. I had always imagined myself as a stay at home mum, doing lots of fun things together with her. I mean, don't get me wrong, Chloe and I still do things together, just not as often as I would like. Sebastian thought it was important for us to have a nanny as we entertained guests quite often, and that meant me spending most of my day in the kitchen cooking, and presenting a spotless home.

I still hadn't heard anything from Sebastian. He was obviously missing my presence! 'Sod him!' I thought 'Why should I spend my time worrying about him, when he isn't giving me a second thought?' I decided to take the bull by the horns and ring Jensen. I'd ring him and invite him for dinner at my hotel. The hotel I was staying in boasted a fine dining experience in Butlers Restaurant, well that's what it said in the brochure! I took the piece of paper, with Jensen's phone number on it, from my handbag and started to dial his number. My hands were shaking and I felt very nervous, as I'd never done anything like this before. I heard Jensen's voice at the other end of the telephone, his voice sounded very sexy. 'Well, it's now or never!' I thought to myself, as I took the plunge and invited him to dinner. I eagerly awaited his response. I couldn't believe it, he replied that he would love to join me, and we arranged to meet up at 7 O'clock in the hotel's library for pre-dinner drinks. God, I couldn't wait! I literally ran back to my room to spend the afternoon pampering myself.

First, I took a long soak in the bath. I'd gone overboard with the bath essence, but what the hell, I deserved it! I then spent an hour doing my hair, putting it up and teasing some of my hair at the side so that it looked curly. People often commented on how much younger I looked with my hair like that. 'Now for my outfit.' I thought. I wanted something that wasn't too overstated, but not too casual. 'What should I wear?' I pondered. After several dress changes, I decided on a classic black Dior dress, which I topped off with a pair of stilettos, and a pearl necklace and earrings. I looked at myself in the full length mirror, glancing over my body. I couldn't remember the last time I'd actually took notice of my figure. I still had my curvaceous, hour-glass figure, even if I had put on a bit of extra weight. I didn't have any wrinkles or laughter lines, probably as I hadn't had much to smile about over the past few years. Although I wasn't a supermodel, I wasn't in that bad a shape. Maybe I could be classed as still fanciable by someone, perhaps that someone could be Jensen! What was I saying? I seemed to have turned into some kind of brazen hussy. Why did I want to feel attractive to Jensen? Oh! My head was spinning. Things felt so mixed up, I didn't know who I was anymore, or what I was turning into!

At ten minutes to seven I made my way downstairs to the library. It was just starting to get busy. I went and sat by the fireplace with its roaring fire. I positioned myself in one of the huge leather armchairs and ordered a gin and tonic, to calm my nerves. Within a few minutes of sitting down I heard Jensen telling the Maître d that 'He was meeting someone here.' 'Yes.' I thought, 'It's me, me, me! God, Calm yourself!' I told myself, as Jensen was shown over to me. He looked really handsome in his black suit. I didn't expect to see him so well dressed, especially since seeing him in his scruffy denims on the plane. He certainly scrubbed up well! We ordered some drinks and Jensen told me how pleased he was to get my phone call. He said that he'd thought about ringing me, but didn't want to come on too strongly, as I'd enough to deal with. 'Well Jensen, if you only knew what I was thinking on the plane. How much I wanted to ravish you, now who would have been coming on too strong? Possibly me?' I thought.

Jensen had the most beautiful eyes, I was transfixed by them. They were very expressive and lit up whenever he smiled. My eyes glanced down to his mouth. He had very sensuous lips, very kissable! I was captivated at the things he was saying, and hung on to every word with anticipation. It felt so good to see him again and I didn't want the night to end. At the dinner table we ordered oysters for starters, and Chateau Briand for the main meal, selecting a bottle of Chardonnay to wash it all down with. The food was cooked to perfection, and the wine was chilled, and heavenly. We talked throughout the meal, and when it came to ordering desserts, we were the only couple left in the restaurant. We must have been there for hours! They do say that time flies when you're having fun! We ordered strawberries and cream for dessert......and another bottle of wine! I was starting to feel quite tipsy. People say that alcohol dulls the senses, but all it did was heighten mine, and every time Jensen took a bite of his strawberries, it sent a tingle down my spine. I hadn't thought watching someone eat could be so sensual, but it certainly was! We finished off the meal by ordering coffee, which we took in the lounge. As the pianist was still playing, Jensen asked me for a dance. He led me to the dance floor, where he pulled me close to him, and led me round the floor. He had actually surprised me. My first impression of Jensen was that he was a bit rough around the edges. He was actually quite well educated, and it just reinforced the saying, never judge a book by its cover.

Jensen pulled me even closer to him, and with my body pressing against his, I began to feel on fire. It was so erotic, my body wanted to feel him closer. I put my head against his broad chest and I could hear his heart beating faster and faster. It was at that point that I knew he wanted me too! Once the pianist stopped playing, Jensen looked into my eyes, and gently cupped my face. I offered my lips to him, and he kissed me. We could both feel the sexual tension between us, we both wanted more and needed to be closer. Jensen took my hand, and we made our way to my room. I had been longing for this moment since I first met him on the plane. He took my room key and unlocked the door. Leaning gently forward, he whispered into my ear. 'Is this what you really want?' He asked. 'Ooh, yes.' I replied instantly. He picked me up and carried me towards the side of the bed. As we stood and gazed at each other, Jensen leant forward and his lips met mine. He kissed me, softly at first, then with an urgency as his animal instinct kicked in! His breath was warm against my lips. He started slowly kissing my neck and I could feel my body aching. Every part of my body felt alive with his touch. I ran my fingers through his hair, my tongue exploring his ears. He gasped with pleasure as I unbuttoned his shirt, and kissed his broad chest. His nipples were hard with excitement as I kissed and tongued them. Jensen slowly removed my dress, letting out a moan of excitement as his eyes fell towards my highly aroused breasts, encased in a black lace basque. Jensen gently cupped my breasts, and explored them with his mouth. I let out a groan of pleasure as his hands moved down over my abdomen, to my groin. 'Ooh! This feels so good!' I thought. 'I haven't been this turned on for such a long time.' Was this what I'd been missing? Every part of my body ached in anticipation of his next touch. I undid Jensen's trousers, and gently stroked his stomach. My lips followed, and I explored his throbbing penis with my mouth. He pulled my face closer to him as I tasted his sexuality. He tasted so good! He knelt down in front of me and parted my legs to reveal my moist, throbbing lips. He began to taste me, as I had him. I felt a wave of emotion, so powerful, that I exploded into his mouth. Finally I'd had my release, and my head was spinning. Jensen carried me onto the bed and slowly, with gentleness, he made love to me. My body felt electric, and every nerve ending I possessed, burned with desire. I sat up and straddled Jensen's body, moving rhythmically back and forth until Jensen cried out as he exploded his seeds of love into my aching groin. We lay holding each other close, not wanting to move too far from each other, enjoying the moment. Tonight we had taken a risk but it had been worth it. This was where I wanted to be, here with Jensen, without a care in the world, and without a thought for Sebastian. Jensen had unearthed something so strong inside of me, so much more than Sebastian and I had shared, and so much more contented. My old life in London seemed a million miles away. My only thought of London was that I'd left my daughter there. I knew I had my responsibilities and I intended to keep them, but for tonight I just wanted to bask in the moment, and the feeling of being needed, and wanted by Jensen! Nothing could spoil this feeling of satisfaction, fulfilment, and warmth. This, to me, felt like home. As we lay in bed holding each other tightly we drifted off to sleep.

The next morning when I awoke I wondered if it had all been a beautiful dream. Had I really spent the night with a handsome and caring man? I turned over to find Jensen lying next to me, and realised that I hadn't been dreaming. I snuggled up closer to Jensen who was still sleeping. The sound of him breathing made me feel quite secure. I nuzzled his back, between his shoulder blades, he smelt heavenly, a combination of his aftershave and his natural body scent. I hadn't taken much notice of people's body scent before, but Jensen's was rather appealing. It must have been something to do with his animal magnetism! I mean, they say we originate from animals, right? I liked the feeling of warmth I got from being laid next to someone that I lusted and had begun to care about. Did I say care about? God I must have it bad! I know it sounds sad, but I was beginning to fall in love with Jensen. I found him funny, charming, sexy, understanding, and did I forget to mention, a real hunk! That of course helped things enormously. We must have laid there with our bodies entwined for another couple of hours. I didn't want to move from his side, so I rang room service and ordered croissants, Danish pastries, yoghurts, and fresh orange juice. I was famished and could have eaten a horse.

Jensen was still asleep when breakfast arrived. It seemed such a shame to wake him, so I set the breakfast out on the table for us to eat later, and headed for the bathroom to take a shower. The water was hot against my skin and quite invigorating. I turned around to get the shower gel, and was greeted by Jensen, wearing nothing but a big smile! He stepped into the shower behind me, and began to rub the shower gel all over my body. The gel began to lather on my body, it felt like I'd been touched with a piece of silk. I'd never experienced such an erotic feeling before and it sent shivers down my spine, and it wasn't long before my body began to react to Jensen's touch. He lathered my back and stomach before slipping his hands between my thighs. He began to tease me with his probing fingers, rubbing gently on my clitoris, my lips began to swell with desire and I began to feel moist. I cried out in ecstasy as I climaxed, shooting my love juice all over his hand. I began to massage the soapy lather around Jensen's groin. His penis became harder with each stroke, moaning and groaning as he came into my hand. Once he'd emptied himself, he stood behind me, took hold of my hands and guided them to my breasts. He encouraged me to touch and massage my-self, rubbing his juices into my breasts. I could feel my nipples beginning to go hard and I cried out with pleasure. Jensen continued to guide my hands all over my body, until I reached my pussy. I started to rub myself, on the verge of exploding I slipped my fingers into my moist vagina. Jensen's manhood started to get hard again, as he rubbed himself against my bottom. He encouraged me to keep playing with myself, and on the verge of orgasm, he bent down and caught my juices in his mouth. He tilted me forwards and took me from behind, frantically pushing his swollen cock into my gaping love hole, and within a few moments, we climaxed together.

Once we'd rinsed each other off, we each wrapped ourselves in a soft towel to get dried. As we reached the bedroom, there was a knock at the door so Jensen went to answer it. It was room service with the champagne he had ordered. As we tucked into our breakfast and sipped our champagne, I started giggling at something Jensen had said, and accidently spilled some champagne on my leg. Jensen leant forward and started kissing my leg. I returned the compliment by kissing around his groin, whilst having the champagne in my mouth. If you ever want to give your man a treat, I recommend you give him lip service like this, It drives them wild!

After breakfast, Jensen and I decided to take in the sights, so we took a trip to Cape Cod, Massachusetts. Boasting more than five hundred miles of unspoilt shorelines, stretching from the quaint village of Falmouth By The Sea, to Provincetown at the tip of the cape, Cape Cod made for a beautiful day out. I loved the look of the rows of clapboard houses and village shops, where everyone made you feel welcome. The charming 'Artists Haven' of Provincetown, was especially worth a visit. It was so nice to share Jensen's company! We went on to visit a place called Hyannis, which was where the Kennedy family retreated to their summer haven, which was now the home of the JFK Memorial and museum. After lunch, Jensen and I strolled along the unspoilt shoreline, with its miles of beaches, sand dunes, wild grasses, pine forests, and heath. It felt very romantic, walking along, holding each other's hand. We eventually made our way back to the hotel. Jensen explained that he had some things to do, and would see me the following day. My heart sank a bit as I didn't want to let him go. Did he think I was just a one night stand? Oh, I hoped not, it was more than just a one night stand for me. Jensen saw the expression on my face. He could tell that I was upset and tried to reassure me, that he would see me the next day, but I wasn't convinced. I had let this man into my life and I was feeling frightened and vulnerable, scared that it was all about to come crashing down around my feet. I took a deep breath and put on a brave smile as I waved Jensen goodbye. 'Only time will tell!' I thought, as I walked through the entrance of the hotel.

When I got back to my room I called Chloe. It was good to hear her voice. She always managed to put a smile on my face no matter what. I missed Chloe terribly. Chloe had been to a party at the house next door to her grandparents house. She had won a prize in one of the party games that they'd played. I imagined her cute, smiling face, beaming with such joy at her achievement. Chloe told me that she had to go, as her new friend was waiting for her in the garden. As always, Chloe finished off her sentence by telling me that she loved me, and would it be alright if she chatted again tomorrow, as they were just about to play their favourite dressing up game! Kids eh? I was pleased that Chloe had made a new friend, perhaps one day she would get to meet my new friend, Jensen!

Once I'd finished my call to Chloe, I rang Charlotte, as she'd promised to be in touch, but I hadn't heard from her. I managed to speak to her, and we arranged to meet up for dinner the following day. I spent the rest of the evening in my hotel room, relaxing. I hadn't walked as far as I had with Jensen, in ages and my feet were supporting two nice blisters. As I lay on the bed my thoughts turned to Charlotte. I was looking forward to seeing her, but I was a little apprehensive about telling her about Jensen, as Charlotte had always got on well with Sebastian, in fact. he was very upset when she decided to take the job in America. I decided to play it by ear and see how things went, before revealing all my dirty secrets. I might even get to hear about her latest conquest. I wondered if Charlotte would ever get married as she had a habit of falling for Mr wrong. You know the type, married with kids and with no intention of leaving their wife. I felt sorry for Charlotte in a way. She must get lonely, waiting around for those men to call, if they called at all! Maybe she had a fear of commitment, who knows. I couldn't understand why someone like Charlotte didn't have someone to come home to. She was beautiful, with long Auburn hair, and a stunning figure! Admittedly she had bought her figure. New boobs, perfect new teeth, and lots of liposuction! 'Ah!' you're saying to yourself, 'A teeny bit jealous are you?' Not at all, it was just that since Chloe was born my priorities had changed somewhat. The thought of spending thousands to make myself more attractive to the opposite sex was ludicrous. I believe that you are what you are, and you just have to make the best of it.

When Charlotte and I were younger, we used to talk about growing up and where we could see ourselves in years to come. Charlotte had said that she wanted at least three kids. I wondered what had changed. I suppose the one thing I wished now was that I still worked and had my own income, instead of being given handouts from my spouse! When I left school I secured work in a bank. I'd worked there for about fifteen years, until I met Sebastian. I'd worked as a personal business banker, Sebastian had come to work at the same bank as 'Head of Corporate Accounts'. We hit it off straight away. Yes, it was love at first sight for me, and after dating for two years, Sebastian had asked me to marry him. Things were going fine until we'd been married for a year when, out of the blue, Sebastian came home one day and announced that he didn't think I should work anymore. Sebastian told me that, As his job was becoming more demanding, and as we were hosting more and more informal business dinners at our house, my main role should be to stay at home to make our lives run like clockwork! After several months of constant emotional blackmail, I finally gave in to his ideas, and peace fell on our house once more. Thinking about it all, I now realised that as long as Sebastian was getting his own way, peace would be bestowed on the homestead, but dare to disagree with one of his decisions and all hell would break loose, and he'd remain in a mood until I finally caved in. I learnt pretty quickly to just conform, as it made my life easier, and to a certain degree, happier. As I drifted off to sleep, my thoughts turned to Jensen, and the magical night we had spent together, and hoped that he was being truthful about ringing me the next day.

The following morning I rose early as I'd booked to go on one of the activities that the hotel had arranged. I was embarking on a five mile hike and was to say the least, apprehensive, as I wasn't the most fit person on the planet. I took a quick shower and pulled on a pair of jeans and a top, and made my way down to breakfast. I wasn't really that hungry but I knew that I should eat something, especially as I would need the energy for the ambitious hike ahead of me.

Our hiking party was to meet in the hotel lobby and by the look of the rest of the group, I wasn't the only one, who would need all the help they could get! Our hike took us past Burlington University, which was where Charlotte worked. I looked to see if I could catch a glimpse of her amongst the hustle and bustle of people on the campus, but I couldn't. The scenery was breathtaking and although my feet hurt, and I didn't relish the prospect of my already blistered feet getting more blistered, I was glad that I'd decided to come on the hike as it gave me a chance to clear my head and get a bit fitter. I'd always promised myself that I would start to get more in shape than I was, but I kept coming up with excuse after excuse, and in the end nothing ever came of it. Perhaps I'd needed a motive, and keeping up with Jensen's sexual appetite had certainly provided the motive! Don't get me wrong, I wasn't complaining, far from it!

We stopped off at a lovely small café for lunch, where they served fish, fish that had been caught and landed that morning. The fish was absolutely beautiful, each forkful just melted in my mouth, divine! I decided to be really naughty and finish off with blueberry pancakes. I know my intention was to get fitter and healthier, but since I'd arrived in America I couldn't help indulging in the food as everything that I'd tasted had been cooked beautifully. I suppose the saying about food cooked for you always tasting better than food you cooked yourself was true. Maybe it was a combination of the quality of the food, and the fact that you were being served it as opposed to serving it yourself.

As we headed back to the hotel, on the final leg of our hike, I got chatting to a couple from Scotland, Mary and Jim. They told me that it was the seventh year in a row that they had stayed at the hotel. They had initially booked the hotel for their honeymoon seven years ago. Apparently both of them had been married before but each had lost their first spouses to cancer. Mary told me that they'd met at a cancer support group that they'd gone to after losing their respective partners, they got chatting and started to help each other through the awful times that followed. Eventually Jim had invited her to lunch, and it all went on from there. I liked Mary and Jim, they were so down to earth and had such likeable personalities. They were very warm and welcoming. I'd promised to meet them for dinner the following night, it was their wedding anniversary. I had said that I didn't want to impose, but they insisted. I think secretly that they felt sorry for me, as I was on my own in the hotel.

We arrived at the hotel. I returned to my hotel room and unlocked the door. The phone was ringing so I answered it. It was Charlotte, finally! She was just ringing to check the evenings arrangements, and that it was still alright to meet up. I said 'Course it was.' And told her that I was looking forward to catching up on all the gossip. Charlotte told me that she was cooking chicken casserole for dinner, and asked if I could bring some wine. I finished my telephone call with Charlotte, and headed straight for the bathroom, where I soaked my aching and blistered feet. Every muscle in my legs ached and I was feeling so tired. After a long soak in the bath, I decided to take a short nap, and as soon as my head hit the pillow, I was in the land of nod.

I awoke from my slumber feeling surprisingly refreshed and energetic, so much so, that I decided to walk to Charlotte's. Just as I made my way through my hotel room door, the phone rang once more. I expected it to be Charlotte, asking me if I minded takeaway as she'd burnt the food. Charlotte wasn't exactly a domestic goddess in the kitchen! To my surprise it wasn't Charlotte, it was Jensen. Well he had promised to ring me, and now he had. Ooh goody! Jensen asked me if he could come and see me, but I told him that I'd already made plans to go and see my friend, Charlotte. We arranged to meet the following day, to spend the day together. I was so relieved that Jensen had rung, I'd been worrying in vain! Perhaps he was one of the good guys, someone who made promises and kept them. Although I felt like putting Charlotte off until another day, so that I could see Jensen, I didn't think it would be fair on Charlotte, especially as she was the reason why I had come to America. I'd just have to be content in the knowledge that I was going to see him the following day. I embarked on my walk to Charlotte's, and felt like I was walking on air. It's a funny thing, this being in lust! Although I felt very close to Jensen, and knew that I was starting to fall for him in a big way, I didn't want to leave myself open to disappointment, especially as I hoped that we would start to see each other more often. Until I knew where we were going with this situation, I didn't want to count all my chickens before they'd hatched.

CHAPTER 3

I arrived at Charlotte's earlier than we'd arranged, the door was slightly open, so I walked inside, to find Charlotte on the phone yet again. She was explaining to whoever was on the other end of the phone, that I had arrived in town to see her. 'It must be another one of Charlotte's boyfriends.' I thought to myself. Charlotte had always done well out of her boyfriends. I remember her telling me that one of her boyfriends had bought her a variety of expensive diamond jewellery, lucky sod! Charlotte caught sight of me, told the other person at the end of the phone she had to go, and quickly put down the receiver. She appeared very flustered, worried that I'd overheard her conversation. I just put it down to her being a very private person. No doubt I would eventually get to hear about her latest beau when she was ready to tell me. I think Charlotte had to feel that the time was right, as she had often told me that she was frightened to go into detail about her boyfriends, as she knew how strongly

I felt about fidelity in a marriage and most of Charlotte's boyfriends in the past had been married. I never once judged her. She was to me, the best friend in the whole wide world so why would I? I often told her to be careful as I didn't want her to get hurt, but judge her, never. Quite frankly, I couldn't really say much at the moment about fidelity in a marriage as I wasn't exactly a good role model following my adultery with Jensen.

The dinner was surprisingly good, and Charlotte's culinary skills had certainly improved since the last time I had tasted her cooking. Well, to be fair, it was about five years ago! After dinner we embarked on the vast amount of washing up that was left. Charlotte must have used every pan she owned, but I couldn't complain. She had excelled herself with the meal. With the dishes done, we settled down on the big comfy sofa, and I started to tell her about my hearing Sebastian's phone call, and that he'd often spend nights away at our city apartment. She asked me why I had finally jumped on a plane to visit her after she had, on numerous occasions, invited me over to see her, but had never come? I had told her that I just needed to see her, after all, we were best friends weren't we?

Charlotte seemed to be distant towards me. I couldn't put my finger on it, but having known her for such a long time I was able to read her. I knew her moods and knew when something was wrong. Maybe it was because we hadn't seen each other for over a year, and that she felt differently about us, but I did feel it was more than that. My intuition was telling me so. Yes, something was definitely different, as Charlotte seemed to be uncomfortable in my presence and rather preoccupied. However as the night went on, Charlotte seemed to get more relaxed, maybe it had something to do with the three bottles of wine that we'd consumed! We began reminiscing about the old days, the times we'd had before she'd moved to America and taken her present job. We were laughing about our dress sense back in the eighties when we used to dress in the style of the new romantics, lots of curly hair and frills.

We had both idolised Simon le bon of Duran Duran, and once went to see them, queuing for hours just for the tickets. We donned our oversized, white dinner shirts, with miniskirts, and belts, God, I could just picture how we looked. Then there was the time that Charlotte started going out with a guy called Kevin. He was mad on snooker, and had his snooker cue permanently 'glued' to his hand. Needless to say that relationship didn't last long, as Charlotte couldn't compete with his love of his snooker cue, it appeared to be a love triangle, with the snooker cue winning! Charlotte reminded me about the time I was serenaded by a guy called Terry. It would have been quite a romantic gesture, had it not been for the fact that he sang outside the wrong bedroom window, and was met by my angry father shouting out of his window at him. Needless to say, that relationship didn't last long!

We opened another bottle of wine and proceeded to get the photo album out. We did laugh, we laughed so much that the tears started to roll down our faces. The conversation then turned to my meeting Sebastian. Charlotte said I was lucky to have landed such a good catch. 'Good catch?' I thought. Having my heart ripped out of my body, when I found out about his affair, didn't make him seem like a good catch to me. I knew Charlotte had always carried a torch for Sebastian, so I didn't think telling her about Jensen would be an appropriate move to make at the present time. I decided that I ought to keep that little indiscretion to myself for a while. I glanced at my watch, it was 12 O'clock, so I decided to call it a night. I wanted to get some beauty sleep before my meeting with Jensen, tomorrow. I had a feeling that I might be nursing a very big hangover, and would need to recuperate before my big date. Charlotte had to call me a cab, as I could hardly stand. I couldn't recall the last time I'd consumed such a large amount of alcohol, mind you, I'd thoroughly enjoyed myself. It had been nice to spend some girly time with Charlotte and catch up with things.

I got back to my hotel and managed to find, and get into, my room. Once inside, I took a couple of headache tablets with a large glassful of water, in the hope of warding off any potential hangover. I crawled into bed and fell straight to sleep. I awoke the next morning to a gentle tapping on my hotel room door. I looked at the clock and saw that it was only 8 O'clock. I wondered who it could be at that time of the morning. I knew it couldn't be Charlotte as, like me, she would still be in bed nursing a hangover! I paused awhile, wondering if I'd got the strength to answer the door. The gentle tapping continued, so I decided to answer the door as the tapping wasn't making my headache any better! Standing at my hotel room door was Jensen, grinning broadly and holding a breakfast tray in one hand. I was surprised to see him at such any early hour. I invited him in, he explained that he'd been unable to sleep as he couldn't wait to see me. I followed him to the table, where he handed me a lovely bunch of flowers. 'I picked these for you as I walked over here to see you.' He told me, smiling broadly like the cat that got the cream. 'What a lovely gesture.' I thought. I much preferred handpicked flowers like those Jensen had brought me, to those big bouquets you can get. The flowers Jensen had picked had been picked with thought, and not just slung together in an over-expensive bouquet. I kissed him on the cheek and thanked him. He turned to me and told me that I looked a bit under the weather, boy was he right! I told him about my evening with Charlotte and the amount of alcohol that we had consumed. Jensen told me that he was going to look after me and beckoned me to sit in the chair by the table. He gave me a cup of strong tea, and lightly buttered a piece of toast, which I refused, but Jensen told me to try and eat something, as I would feel a lot better! As I ate my breakfast, Jensen went into the bathroom to run me a hot bath. He came into the bedroom to see if I had finished eating, and then took my hand and led me to the bathroom. I took off my bathrobe and climbed into the bath of bubbles. 'Ah, that feels better.'

I thought as the hot water soothed my body. Jensen picked up the soap and gently washed my body. 'He has such a soft touch' I thought to myself, as he massaged my shoulders with the soapy lather. He leaned forward and kissed my neck. 'Oh I don't know if I'm up to a morning of passion.' I thought, but Jensen didn't touch me sexually, he touched me tenderly, with care and attention. His goal wasn't to get me aroused but to look after, and relax me. How many men would have took advantage of the situation and tried to seduce me even though I wasn't feeling my best? After my bath I went and laid back on my bed where Jensen handed me a glass of water and some tablets. Then he went into the bathroom to wet a facecloth, which he placed gently on my forehead. Jensen then clambered onto my bed, fully clothed, and held me in his arms whilst I drifted off to sleep once again. I must have slept for hours as the sun had moved round to the side window of my room. 'Are you feeling better?' Jensen asked. I nodded, 'Good, then I'll go and get you something to eat.' He replied.

I told him to order room service, but he insisted that he would go and choose something for me himself. While Jensen was out getting some food I managed to get up and put on some clothes, nothing too glamorous, just a casual dress. Within a few minutes Jensen returned, clutching a tray filled with cakes, sandwiches and fresh fruit. As we tucked into the food I thanked Jensen for all his help. He told me not to be so silly, as he was only looking after me, anyone would have done the same. 'Oh how wrong he was! Sebastian wouldn't have been so considerate.' I thought. I remembered a time that I'd come down with flu. It happened to coincide with yet another dinner party that we were hosting. I wanted Sebastian to cancel and re-schedule it for another day, a time when I would be feeling better, but Sebastian wouldn't hear of it, so I had to muddle on, and as always, play the perfect hostess.

Jensen asked if I felt up to going out as he had something that he wanted to show me. I asked what it was but he wanted to keep it a secret. As I felt much better, I agreed to accompany him. It's surprising how well you feel when you've been shown kindness and attention. I was looking forward to seeing where he was taking me. Jensen ordered a cab, Jensen handed the driver a piece of paper. The cab driver set off, and started heading out of town, and into the countryside. The cab stopped at a small bridge and we climbed out. I looked around but I still hadn't a clue where he was taking me.

Jensen pointed into the distance, towards a house, and declared 'That's where we're heading.' We walked down a narrow lane that led up to the house. It was beautiful. Someone had obviously been renovating it. I asked Jensen who it belonged to, and to my surprise Jensen told me it was his. He led me onto the front porch, where there was a small wooden table and chairs. On a table, stood a vase of wild flowers. Jensen proceeded to open the front door which led into a large living room boasting an open fire. The wooden floors were highly polished. The room only had a couple of leather sofas and a coffee table, and although there was a lack of furniture, the house looked homely and well cared for. Looking round at the house I noticed the wonderful craftsmanship that had gone into it.

Jensen had told me that he had carried out all the work himself. From the living room I was led to the master bedroom which had a big wrought iron bed in the centre. One wall was full of floor to ceiling wardrobes which had been crafted to a high standard. A small doorway in the bedroom led to an en-suite bathroom. The en-suite featured a roll top bath in the centre of the room with the W.C. and a wash hand basin in one corner. The next room I was shown was a guest bedroom, again with floor to ceiling wardrobes. The main bathroom was yet to be finished, but the walls and paintwork had been done and the bathroom suite was still waiting to be fitted.

The final room I was shown was a huge kitchen. Whitewashed cabinets and shelves were fitted on every one of the walls, with a large, ceramic butler sink and hand carved worktops complementing the units. It was beautiful. I would have bought the house myself. It had a pleasant atmosphere which filled each room. 'This house would make someone a happy home' I thought to myself. The back of the house featured a second porch, and beyond that were fields full of wild flowers that stretched as far as the eye could see. I loved it! Jensen told me that he had purchased the land a couple of years earlier while he had been working in America. He'd always intended to live there full time, eventually, and he started renovating the house eight months ago. He explained that his mother was American and lived in Stowe whilst his father originated from Hove, England. His parents had separated when he was ten years old, so over the last twenty five years he'd lived between both countries, spending time equally with each of his parents. Jensen told me that he was a qualified master carpenter, and his house had been a hobby of his, working on it whenever he got the chance.

I knew his hands were skilled, I could tell that by the way he'd touched and caressed my body, and finding that his hands had created such beautiful workmanship didn't really surprise me in the least. We went and sat on the back porch where Jensen opened a wicker hamper and pulled out a bottle of champagne and two glasses followed by a bowl of strawberries, which he placed on the table. He handed me a glass of champagne, telling me that he wanted to share this moment with me. He had just about finished renovating the house except for 'plumbing in' the main bathroom, and wanted to toast the house as this was meant to bring good luck to whoever lived there. Jensen leant forward and kissed my lips, his kiss sent shivers down my spine. He kissed my neck and his hands skimmed over my dress to my breasts. I gasped in pleasure as my body began to throb with desire. Jensen continued to skim over my dress with his hands, until he reached my thighs. He lifted the hem of my dress and placed his hand on my briefs. He started to stroke his hand up and down over my briefs and I could feel myself beginning to get wet between my legs. He pulled my briefs to one side and slowly slipped his fingers into me. He began to stimulate my clitoris and with a steady hand brought me to orgasm. Then he knelt in front of me and lifted up my dress. He slipped off my briefs to reveal my highly aroused body. He gently kissed my thighs and lips, before sucking my clitoris, sending waves of passion through my body as I cried out his name. He slowly unbuttoned my dress and it slipped off, falling onto the floor in a silken pile.

His hands mapped my body, exploring every part of me once more. He picked me up and carried me into his bedroom and placed me gently on the bed. I unbuttoned his shirt and kissed his neck and shoulders, my tongue tracing a path towards his stomach. I undid his jeans, pulled them off and threw them to the floor. His penis was fully erect and I began to tease him with my tongue. I then slid his penis into my mouth and gently sucked on him. I started to gently rub my teeth up and down him and Jensen began to moan. I could feel his manhood pulsating in my mouth. He laid back onto the bed and I kissed his abdomen and sides, my mouth continued, first down one leg to his ankle, then back up the other leg. All the time Jensen flinching and groaning with pleasure, as I made my way up to his balls. I gently licked and sucked at his balls, listening intently to his moans and groans. The more intense his moans became, the more I kissed, sucked and licked him.

I asked Jensen to turn over onto his stomach, and started to kiss his shoulders and back. I licked a path with my tongue to his buttocks, caressing them with my hands and tongue. I licked around his balls and then just below, near his rectum, he quivered uncontrollably as I worked on him. From his reactions, I knew he found it exciting! Jensen turned over and parted my legs, he got on top of me and entered me slowly. I needed him to make love to me hard, the harder the better. I pulled him further inside me as I dug my nails into his buttocks, our lovemaking got more and more urgent as we both reached orgasm. As we lay holding each other, Jensen started to stroke my face and hair, I couldn't get over how tender he was, and thought how mad his ex-fiancé must have been to let him go. I felt very safe in his arms and I held onto him, not wanting to let him go. Her loss was my gain. Jensen asked me where I thought our friendship was going, it was a question I'd asked myself many times since meeting him. I didn't know what to say, I didn't want to just blurt out that I wanted him and needed him to be by my side forever, in case he felt differently. 'What do you want from this?' I asked him. 'To be with you' he replied. 'Thank you, lord!' I thought, casting my eyes heavenwards.

Maybe, just maybe, this could work out. I explained to Jensen that I'd come to America to sort my life out, to see if I could salvage my relationship with Sebastian, but having met him, things had changed. I no longer saw a future with Sebastian. I didn't want to settle for second best anymore, Jensen had made me realise that I could have happiness in my life, and Jensen was the one who made me happy. I told Jensen that I had no wish to return home to England. I wanted to stay there with him. He said 'Why don't you stay then?' 'I can't leave Chloe!' I told him. 'Why don't you bring Chloe to America, and we'll live together as a family?' Jensen suggested. 'I wish it was that simple, but Sebastian wouldn't let me bring Chloe to America. Not that he would want her full time, it would be because I was taking one of his possessions away from him! To Sebastian, Chloe and I are both his possessions!' I explained. Jensen responded by telling me that, if we both wanted it badly enough, we would find a way to be together, and Jensen wanted us to be here! Tears started to well up in my eyes. I was scared that this was all a dream and I would wake up and fall back down to earth with a bang. Never in my life had someone so wonderful, loved me the way he did. Never in my life had someone wanted me so much.

I'd learned early on in life that everything came at a cost, and I was worried what living in complete happiness would cost me. Jensen turned my face towards his and wiped away the tears from my eyes. 'Don't cry, I'll take care of you forever' he told me. Then he kissed my eyelids and nose and gave me a sexy smile. For the first time in my life, I'd found someone I trusted in, I knew Jensen's words weren't cheap and I believed in him. We lay together on the bed until it got dark. I told Jensen that I'd agreed to meet Mary and Jim that evening, as they were celebrating their wedding anniversary and I'd been invited to dine with them.

Jensen suggested that I should get back to the hotel, and he called me a cab. Jensen asked if he could see me the following day, I told him that I didn't want to wait that long to see him, and I invited him to accompany me and have dinner with Mary and Jim too. I'd just found him and wasn't going to let him go that easily!

Jensen took a shower then put on his suit, just as the cab pulled up. We headed back to the hotel so that I could freshen up before meeting up with Mary and Jim for dinner. As we arrived at the hotel, I spotted Mary at the reception desk. I introduced her to Jensen and asked if they would mind if Jensen joined us. 'Not at all' Mary replied, giving me an approving wink. I told Mary that we'd only be about half an hour, and that we would meet them in the library for pre-dinner drinks. In my room I took a quick shower, as I was feeling all hot and sweaty after our afternoon of love-making. I felt so happy and contented, and couldn't believe it. Good things didn't usually happen to me. I dried myself down and put on a pair of tailored trousers and a blouse. Jensen remarked how the trousers hugged my peachy bottom, and how sexy they made me look. I liked looking sexy, but I'd not considered myself sexy for a long time. I could get used to being called sexy! We made our way downstairs to meet Mary and Jim.

Mary and Jim were sat near the library window, and on seeing us, they beckoned us over. I could tell that we were all going to have a pleasant evening. Jim kept us all entertained with stories of when he was a fisherman whilst we waited to be seated at our table. As the time went by Jims stories got taller and taller, Mary kept telling him to shut up, in case he was boring us, but in truth, I found him rather entertaining. He certainly had me in tears of laughter. Jim asked Jensen how long we had known each other, as he turned and winked at me as if to give his seal of approval. The maître d came over and led us to our table. Jensen ordered champagne and told us all to sit back and enjoy ourselves and order what we liked as he was going to take care of the bill as it was such a special occasion. Mary told Jensen that he didn't need to do that but Jensen insisted. I turned and mouthed the words 'Thank you' to Jensen who, in returned mouthed the words 'No problem!' and gave me one of his sexy smiles. I chose an Asparagus starter, followed by Duck in Blackcurrant Sauce for the main course. Jensen ordered the Seafood Platter and Sirloin Steak, whilst Mary and Jim both ordered Prawn Cocktails for starters and Chicken Chasseur for the main course. We sat happily chatting as we all ate our food, I was really enjoying myself. When it came to ordering desserts, we all decided that we were too full to eat anything else. We decided to take coffee in the lounge, and as the waiter organised this we made our way to the big comfy sofas in the lounge. Jensen sat next to me and placed his hand on my knee. I could feel my pulse start to race as he settled back into the leather sofa and started chatting to Jim.

I watched Jensen as he engaged in conversation, he was so handsome. I loved the way his eyes lit up as he laughed, and he had the most perfect smile. I couldn't stop looking at him, just listening to him talk gave me goose bumps! Mary caught me looking at him and gave me a wry smile. I felt embarrassed having been caught drooling over him. 'You ought to hang on to that one, he seems a good un' said Jim, while Jensen was away taking care of the bill. I felt myself blush, but Jim's comments filled me with pride. Mary said that she could tell Jensen was smitten with me as he had that look, 'In fact you both have that look!' She told me. Jensen returned and asked if we wanted to join him on the dance floor. Mary jumped up and grabbed Jensen's arm and proceeded to march him to the dance floor. Jim took my arm and we followed them.

The hotel had booked a singer who kept us entertained with songs like 'I'd rather go blind' by Chicken Shack, from the sixties. When she announced that the next song was for all those lovers out there, and started to sing 'Lady in Red' by Chris De Burgh. Jensen took my hand and pulled me closer to him, the words of the song swam around in my head as I rested my head against his shoulder. As we held each other closer, I could smell the mix of Jensen's aftershave and his natural body scent. It was enough to get me tingling all over. He started to nuzzle my neck and I could feel my body reacting to his touch. I could feel my nipples standing erect, and I began to get moist between my thighs. Jensen heard me moaning and groaning under my breath, and he pulled me even closer. I could feel that Jensen too was in an aroused state, his penis pushing hard against me. I felt as though I was going to pass out as my head spun in anticipation of the night ahead. We bid Mary and Jim goodnight, left the dance floor and headed for my room. We reached the bedroom door, I couldn't wait to get Jensen inside, and not just inside the bedroom! I led him into my room by his tie, and started to remove his jacket. I unbuttoned Jensen's shirt, then proceeded to strip him of his clothes, revealing his beautiful aroused body standing in front of me. I kissed Jensen on the lips letting my tongue trace the line of his mouth, as I did so, Jensen let out a moan of pleasure so I did it again. I began licking a path down his muscular torso, to his groin. I teased and flicked the end of his throbbing manhood with my tongue before taking him in deep into my mouth. Jensen let out a gasp and held my head, pulling it harder against him. I gently stroked his buttocks with my fingers and just as he was on the verge of exploding, I pulled him closer still, by digging my nails into his buttocks. Jensen groaned more and more, finally exploding his seed into my mouth. Jensen started to undress me, first unbuttoning my blouse to reveal my red lace bra, before sliding his hands down my body to the waistband of my trousers, until he reached my trouser zip. I heard the zip undo and my trousers fell to the floor. I stepped out of them and stood in front of Jensen undressed, apart from my red lace French knickers and matching bra. He certainly liked what he saw, as Jensen began to rise to the occasion again. He undid my bra and slipped the straps off my shoulders, throwing it to the floor before taking my breasts in his hands and starting to lick and suck at my nipples. His hands slid over my body with ease, and with such firm hands, Jensen set my senses on fire. Using his teeth, he teased my French knickers from my body before firmly placing his mouth over my pulsating mound. His tongue explored every inch of my pussy with such urgency, that within minutes I had reached orgasm, exploding my cum into his hot mouth. He led me to a chair near the bedroom window and gently bent me over it, before slipping himself into me from behind. He began to make love to me, slowly at first, before quickening the pace, holding onto my thighs as he went faster and faster. I screamed out with desire as Jensen called out my name. 'Arabella, Arabella!' He cried. It drove me wild and I started calling out his name too, Before reaching orgasm in perfect synchronicity. We both collapsed on the floor out of exhaustion and just laid there, holding each other close. Jensen looked lovingly at me and told me that he was falling in love with me and never wanted to let me go. I was in heaven. 'How lucky am I? Jensen felt the same way as I did.' I thought to myself. As we lay there, the phone began to ring. I looked at Jensen and told him that I'd better answer it. I made my way to the phone and picked up the receiver, 'Hello!' I said. 'Arabella! It's Sebastian.' Before I could answer him he added, 'What the hell are you playing at? When are you coming home? I've got the Wilson's coming round for dinner next week, will you be back by then?' He asked. 'Well Sebastian, why do you think I've gone away,?' I replied. 'And anyway, how did you know how to reach me? Did my mum tell you? 'Your mother, What's your mother got to do with this?' Sebastian enquired. I shot Jensen a look and mouthed the word 'sorry' to him. He looked rather embarrassed and made his way to the bathroom.

'So you haven't been in touch with my mum then?' I asked Sebastian. 'No, why should I?' 'Because that is where our daughter is!' I replied, 'You do remember her don't you? Chloe! Four years old!' I remarked sarcastically. 'Chloe's at your mothers!' Sebastian shouted, 'I thought she'd be with you! What's she doing at your mothers?' Sebastian continued. 'My parents are looking after her, I needed to get away for a while.' I replied. 'Look Sebastian, what do you want?' I continued. 'I've just told you Arabella, I've got the Wilson's coming for dinner on Friday and I need you back!' I told him that I wouldn't be back by Friday, and put the phone down on him. I went into the bathroom to see Jensen. He was taking a shower. 'Sorry about that!' I said. 'I wasn't expecting him to phone.' 'Hey look, don't worry about it, maybe I should go so you can sort things out.' Jensen replied. 'I don't want you to go, there's nothing to sort out anyway.' I said. 'He didn't even know Chloe was at my mums, and he didn't even ask why I'd had to get away!' I continued. Jensen said that if Sebastian hadn't been in touch with my mum, how did he know where to find me? 'I don't know! Perhaps he's spoken to Charlotte.' I said.

Jensen put his arms around me and told me that things would work out. To find the answers to my problems, all I had to do was to look into my heart and listen to what it was telling me. I was so annoyed at Sebastian. He was oblivious to everything. He didn't care about me, or our daughter for that matter. He only cared about my role as a dutiful wife. Someone to host his dinner parties! It was too late to phone my mum, so I decided I'd ring her in the morning. I thought I'd ring Charlotte too, to see if Sebastian had rung there. I needed to unwind so I stepped into the hot shower. I always took a bath or shower when I needed to relax. 'Oh! Damn you Sebastian! Damn you for being so you!' I thought. I spent half an hour in the shower, and when I emerged from the bathroom, I found Jensen sat on the side of the bed fully clothed, and looking rather hurt. I knew just how he felt! Sebastian had ruined our perfect evening, and because he had, he'd put a dampener on the whole evening. Now I wasn't sure if I would see Jensen again after tonight. Maybe my life was too complicated for him.

I walked towards the side of the bed and sat beside Jensen. 'I'm so sorry, I had no idea he was going to ring, it's the first time he's rang since I got here.' I told him. 'It's okay, I knew you'd have to speak to him at some point,' he said. 'would you mind if I called a cab?' He continued. I nodded, fearing that I'd just blown the best thing in my life, other than Chloe of course. I ambled into the bathroom and put on my clothes. Within a few minutes of getting dressed, the telephone rang. It was the girl on the reception desk letting me know that Jensen's cab had arrived. I looked longingly at Jensen and asked him if we could meet up again in the morning. He laughed then smiled before telling me that I was being silly if I thought I wouldn't see him again he told me I could see him all night as I was going back to his house to spend the night with him. 'You need a change of scenery and that's the reason I called a cab.' he explained. I've never felt so relieved in all my life. I thought that I'd lost Jensen after tonight's episode! I closed my room door as we headed down the stairs hand in hand, out of the hotel doors to the waiting cab, which we climbed into before setting off for Jensen's house.

CHAPTER 4

We arrived at Jensen's. He opened the front door and ushered me into the living room. He took off my coat and told me to make myself comfortable on the sofa. He went and hung up my coat before returning to the living room. He told me that he was going to make a fire and went outside to get some logs. Jensen came back in after a few minutes and set about making a fire. It didn't take long for the fire to warm the room up, as the logs crackled and spat, and blazed with an intense heat, Jensen asked if I was feeling hungry, to which I replied that I was. Jensen went into the kitchen to see what we could have, returning about fifteen minutes later clutching a tray filled with two platefuls of cheese and toast and two mugs of hot chocolate. It tasted divine. Sometimes even the simplest of foods are the most satisfying, and this was no exception! We cuddled up beside each other, and watched the roaring fire. I now knew what being in heaven was like, and this was my heaven. We lay by the fire until it finished burning, until the last ember had lost its orangey glow. Jensen then led me into his bedroom and undressed me and tucked me up in bed, before clambering in beside me, where we both drifted off to sleep.

The next morning I woke to the sound of singing, it appeared to be coming from the kitchen, so I climbed out of bed, borrowed Jensen's shirt, and made my way into the kitchen. There stood Jensen in his birthday suit making breakfast. I smiled, he hadn't noticed me standing in the doorway! 'I Want to Break Free' by Queen was playing on the radio. Jensen was prancing around the kitchen singing, and I let out a chuckle. Jensen turned round, rather embarrassed, and announced that he'd thought it would be nice if he made me breakfast. I told him that I liked his sexy dance and he shyly blushed then let out a nervous laugh. Jensen took my hand and led me out onto the back porch where he had set the small table with freshly picked wild flowers. On the table freshly squeezed orange juice and croissants waited for me. I sat at the table and Jensen brought out a tray, and on it sat two plates crammed with bacon, eggs, tomatoes and mushrooms. I was suitably impressed! A good looking man who was loving and caring, and to top it all, a man who could cook! I tucked into breakfast, eating until I couldn't eat any more. Jensen's breakfast was delicious, the best breakfast that I'd ever eaten! After breakfast Jensen asked me what I fancied doing for the rest of the day. 'I want to spend the rest of the day in bed with you!' I cheekily replied. Jensen smiled at me and replied 'Why don't we compromise and go out this morning and we'll spend the afternoon and evening in bed' I didn't need much persuasion. I told Jensen that I needed to go back to the hotel for a change of clothes, and I had a couple of calls to make first. We washed the breakfast pots together and got dressed, then made our way back to the hotel.

On our arrival at the hotel, I was given a message telling me that Sebastian had tried to get in touch after I had spoken to him the previous night, and he said that he would try to contact me again later this morning. I decided I'd postpone speaking to Sebastian until I'd found out how he knew where I was and how to contact me. Especially since my mum hadn't told him. Jensen and I headed up the grand staircase to my hotel room. We entered my room and I sat on the edge of my bed. I dialled my mum's number, Chloe answered, 'Mummy, mummy, I'm missing you!' She told me. 'Nanny wants to speak to you so I'll just pass her the phone, bye mummy, I love you.' Chloe continued. My mum came on the phone, 'Hello Arabella, I've had Charlotte on the phone, she was asking some very peculiar questions.' My mum told me. 'Like what?' I replied. 'Well, she was asking if Sebastian had given me a call, and if he had, had he managed to speak to you! I thought you'd seen Charlotte?' My mum said. 'I have, but I've not seen much of her as she told me that she had work commitments. I'm going to ring her later today.' I added. 'Well she sounded in a right state!' My mum replied. I told my mum that I'd call her later, and to give Chloe a big kiss from me, before putting down the phone. After I'd put the receiver down, I sat on the bed. I was rather puzzled and it must have shown as Jensen asked if everything was okay. I told him that I wasn't sure. I tried Charlotte's number. 'It's Arabella, is everything okay?' I asked, as Charlotte picked up the phone. 'I've just been speaking to my mum and she said that you'd phoned her asking if Sebastian had called her, and if he had, did she know if I'd spoken to him, What's going on?' I enquired. Charlotte paused awhile, then told me that she couldn't talk about it on the phone. Then she asked if we could meet up later that evening. I agreed and arranged to go round there at 8 O'clock. I felt that something was definitely going on and maybe tonight I might get to the bottom of it.

I wondered why Charlotte was acting so cagey. I guess I'd find out later that evening, whatever it was. I remembered that I'd arranged to go on a cycling trip at lunchtime and asked Jensen if he fancied joining me or should I cancel it and we could go and do something else. He told me that he hadn't been on a bike since he was a child, but he was game for it. As we still had a couple of hours to kill until we embarked on our cycle ride, we decided to have a walk around the hotel gardens. The gardens were beautiful. They had been divided into different sections, with each section offering to please the senses in a different way. We walked around the scented garden first. As soon as we reached the entrance, we could smell the sweetness of the flowers. The lawns, with their lavender edged borders, brought back memories of my nanna. She always wore lavender toilet water. I could remember every time that I visited her as a child, as I was close to her. She'd often show me how to make presents for people, using the simplest of things. My favourite 'makes' were decorated soaps. My nanna would give me a bar of soap which I'd cover in lace, before putting coloured pins into it, to form pretty patterns. We would finish the soaps off with coloured ribbon, before making boxes out of coloured card, to place them in. The end results were amazing, and very pretty. Tears welled up in my eyes as I thought back to those happy times. I was devastated when my nanna died, I was only fifteen!

On the day of her funeral, I followed her coffin, alongside my parents in the main car. I was heartbroken and beside myself with grief, crying out to my nanna in the hearse in front, telling her that she wasn't allowed to leave me, but she did. Jensen saw that I had tears in my eyes, so he put his arms around my shoulder and asked me if everything was ok? I started to tell him about my nanna. Further along the gardens, we came to my favourite flowers, sweet peas. They were trailing up some trellis next to the garden wall, whilst white alyssum and blue lobelia covered the ground. There were tubs of pansies adorning the paved area, it was breathtaking. If I were to plan a garden from scratch, this would be what I would base it on. We then strolled along to the maze garden, where Jensen dared me to find him. I explained that I had no sense of direction, but would have a go at finding him in the maze. 'Hmm! Hunt the hunk' I thought. But I made Jensen promise that if I hadn't found him in forty five minutes, then he would have to come and find me! I wandered round and round the maze, calling out Jensen's name to no avail. I began to panic as it occurred to me that, not only had I failed to find Jensen, but I'd gone and got myself lost too! I called out to Jensen in a frightened voice. After what seemed like absolutely ages, Jensen appeared behind me laughing. I turned round to Jensen with tears in my eyes, as I'd been scared at the thought of being lost. Jensen could see that I was upset and took me into his arms. Holding me close, he told me not to worry, as no matter where I was he would always find me and keep me safe. We found our way out of the maze and walked down to the lake, just further along the route, and sat on one of the benches beside it, just taking in the fresh air. We put our arms around each other and I held on for dear life. I loved this feeling of security and contentment, and wanted the feeling to last forever! The sun was gleaming down from the sky, it was a glorious day. Jensen laid back on the bench and pulled me towards him, and there we lay, for what we seemed like an hour, me with my head on his chest. It was only when some children playing next to the lake started to splash each other, that we decided to make our way back to the hotel. We arrived at the hotel with just enough time to have a quick cup of coffee before setting off on our cycle ride. I was enjoying myself with Jensen.

It was just nice to take time out and enjoy the beautiful surroundings. It felt like time was standing still and nothing or no one could spoil the time that we were spending together. 'It would be great if everyday could be like this.' I thought. As we descended the stairs to the reception, I heard my name being called. It was the organiser of the cycle ride calling me as I was running slightly late. I explained that Jensen was going to accompany me, and we made our way outside to join the rest of the party, and to collect our bicycles. We had a choice, ladies bicycles or a tandem! I couldn't quite imagine Jensen on a ladies bicycle, so we opted for the tandem. We both clambered aboard the tandem and attempted to ride it. It was quite difficult at first, especially when we had to try and pedal at the same time. Once we'd got the hang of it, we were soon cycling down the country lanes with the rest of the cycling party. We were on our way to visit a small Amish village about two hours away, and although I wasn't exactly enthralled at having to cycle for two hours, I was looking forward to seeing the Amish village. In many ways I thought the Amish way of life was the sort of life I wanted, with the sense of community, and the way they helped each other to build each other's houses and barns. I liked that they believed in living off the land and living simply. The only drawback for me was the lack of electricity, and the appliances that make the day to day chores easier. I couldn't imagine washing everything by hand, especially the daily amount of washing I had to do at home! In an ideal world it would be nice to live amongst each other in peace and harmony, with no wars, famine, illegal drugs, and unnecessary killings. We should all try to find a way to accept everyone's way of life, after all it takes all sorts of people to make a world!' I thought to myself.

As we approached the village, a sense of calm filled the air. The birds were chirping in the trees and I could see the children from the village playing together in the distant fields. On our arrival at the village we were met by one of the 'Elders', who ran the community. He explained that we would be able to see how they lived, and the products they made to sell to the visitors, to help with their income. We were first shown around one of the houses. I couldn't get over how beautiful the house was, all the furniture seemed to be hand carved, the tables and chairs were exceptional. A big open fire adorned the living room wall, which were all painted pale blue. A huge tapestry depicting harvest time, hung on one of the walls. We were led into the kitchen where a group of the womenfolk were busy filling jars with homemade jams and pickles. Jensen was impressed with the craftsmanship of the kitchen, he appreciated the good workmanship, being a carpenter himself. We could see the amount of work that had gone into this kitchen! We were shown around the rest of the house. I was taken aback by the homeliness of the house, for although it was quite sparse, I could quite easily have lived there.

We moved on, to the village church, it was only small, but once inside, it was obvious that the Amish people took pride in everything they did, you could see that just by looking at the rows of hand carved benches. We moved on and were led to a barn that was just being built, all the men of the village were helping to erect the barn. It was nice to see how, with team spirit and enthusiasm, they pulled together to build it.

There were a number of big tables and benches sat on a grassed area to one side of the barn. The women were hurriedly filling the tables with food and drink for their men folk to eat and drink. Once the tables were laden, the women called out to the men, inviting them to eat and drink. We were beckoned over to join them. I surveyed the tables, and looked at the various dishes adorning them. On each table sat plates, with thick slices of cooked ham, and slices of cheese, and a couple of loaves of homemade bread, along with jars of freshly made, homemade jams and pickles, and a bowl of rosy apples sat alongside huge pitchers of homemade lemonade.

As we tucked in to the tremendous feast, the village folk told us about the way they lived their life and about their life principles, which we all found interesting. One man called Tobias had told us of the mixed reactions they receive when they ride into town to get supplies. He told us that some people jeer them, and push and shove the men folk. I couldn't understand why the townspeople would treat them so badly, but Tobias explained that they thought the men folk of the village controlled the women, but in reality, the women just respected their men folk and liked being looked after, without being left to sort out everyday problems. That was a job left to the men. Tobias said that they didn't believe in violence, so they just ignored the people from the towns as best they could and wouldn't stoop to their violent level. I couldn't believe that in today's society, this still happened. I suppose it could be put down to ignorance, but that was still no excuse! After we had eaten, the men went back to work, whilst the women cleared the tables. I offered to help them but they said that we were guests and wouldn't dream of us helping. As everyone was busy, Jensen and I decided to take a walk around the village. It was really refreshing to see all the children playing nicely together, and not falling out or bickering with each other. Chloe would have loved it here!

A little while later one of the women, who was called Marybeth, showed us to a little store room to let us see the patchwork quilts that the women made. They must have spent many hours on each of the quilts as the stitching was very neat and intricate, the women were certainly as talented as the men of the village! It was almost time for us to leave, so I reached into my pocket to offer some money to Marybeth for the lovely lunch we'd eaten, but she just smiled and said that there was no need, as it was just their way of being hospitable. I felt embarrassed that I might have upset her by offering to pay for our food, but we were told that their quilts, jams and pickles were for sale if we wished to buy something. I jumped at the chance, as I'd spotted two quilts that I liked when we'd been shown them earlier. I hadn't a clue as to how I'd get them back to the hotel, but I bought them anyway. I also purchased two jars of strawberry jam, two jars of chutney, and three bottles of Elderflower cordial. I just couldn't resist the temptation to buy them, as they were the best homemade goods that I'd ever tasted. 'Can I pay now, and pick them up later,' I asked, 'It would be a struggle to take my goods, and Jensen, back to the hotel at the same time, and there's no way I'm leaving my Jensen!' I continued. Marybeth laughed, 'That's fine.' She said.

Jensen had paid a visit to the wood store and had bought a couple of items of furniture, but he wouldn't tell me what he'd bought. He told me that it was a surprise, and that he was going to pick them up another day. He laughed when I told him what I'd bought, I think he knew I couldn't resist not buying anything. Our cycling party regrouped and we began to pedal our way back to the hotel. After a couple of hours cycling we arrived at the hotel, saddle sore to say the least! Jensen and I made our way to my hotel room where we both collapsed, absolutely exhausted. I looked at the clock on the bedside table, it said Six-thirty. I was due at Charlotte's at 8 O'clock, but I just didn't have the energy to get ready to go. I told Jensen that I was going to cancel my meeting with Charlotte, and arrange it for another night, but Jensen said that maybe what Charlotte had to tell me was important. I told him that, although I was keen to know what she wanted to tell me, I was too tired to go, and to be honest, I would probably fall asleep which would likely annoy Charlotte. Jensen told me to do what I thought was best, so I proceeded to ring Charlotte. Charlotte picked up the receiver, and I explained that I'd been on a long cycle ride and was shattered. I asked if she would mind if I cancelled our meeting this evening, and rearrange our meeting for another night. Charlotte explained that she needed to talk to me about something important, and the sooner we could talk, the better. I went on to explain that I wasn't up to it, but Charlotte insisted that what she had to tell me really couldn't wait. Reluctantly, I agreed to go round, and put down the telephone receiver. I turned to Jensen who put his hand on my knee and gave it a gentle squeeze, telling me that everything would be fine. Oh how I wished I could believe him, but something in Charlotte's voice made me uneasy. Jensen offered to run me a bath, while I chose the clothes that I was going to wear to Charlotte's. I climbed into the warm bathwater. I could feel all my muscles relaxing with the heat of the water. I've always had a thing about being clean. Whenever anything troubled me, the first thing I would do was to run myself a hot bath to help me unwind, and wash away my fears. It seemed to be the only thing that was able to relax me. Jensen sat on the side of the bath and gently massaged my shoulders, it was bliss! For just a moment, it felt like I'd finally found what I was looking for, in my life.

My search had ended, and I felt complete. I finished taking my bath and stood up to get out of the tub. Jensen stood there with his arms outstretched, holding a warm, fluffy towel. As I stepped from the bath Jensen encased me in a towel. I looked into his beautiful eyes and smiled, and as I did so, tears welled in my eyes. 'Why hadn't I felt this safe and loved before?' I wondered. I felt that all my life I had been putting myself on hold, pleasing everyone else, and not considering my needs! This trip had certainly been an awakening for me, and I knew I couldn't go back to living my life, the way I had previously. Jensen pulled me close and kissed my lips, then he kissed my tears. 'From now on, I only want to see happy tears.' He told me. It was as if he understood how I felt without me having to speak. It was at that moment, I knew that I had found true love, a love that was worth fighting for, whatever the price. All I knew is that Jensen made me feel emotions that I never knew I could feel. He had awakened my soul. I put on my clothes and phoned for a taxi to take me to Charlotte's. I told Jensen that he could wait for me in my room as I wouldn't be long, but he decided that he would go home and see me the next day. The telephone rang, it was the hotel receptionist letting me know that my taxi was waiting for me. We went downstairs and Jensen kissed me and asked me to ring him later.

I nodded and got in the taxi. As the taxi moved away, Jensen disappeared from view, and I felt uncomfortable, I don't know why, maybe I was just feeling nervous about Charlotte's big secret and what it might be. Something inside me told me that I wasn't going to like what Charlotte was going to reveal, it was a sort of sixth sense. I arrived at Charlotte's house and knocked on the door. She sheepishly opened the door. I gave her a hug, but she seemed to freeze on the spot. Perhaps my sixth sense was right after all! Charlotte led me into the lounge and offered me a glass of wine. I cut to the chase and asked Charlotte what our meeting was all about. Charlotte turned to me with tears in her eyes. I told her that things couldn't be that bad, and if it was, I was sure we could put things right together. She let out a sigh, 'I wish it was that simple.' She replied, as she came over and sat next to me on the sofa. 'I've got something to tell you, that you're not going to like.' She said. She began by asking me if I remembered how quickly she'd made the decision to move to America, and take a job she'd been offered, a job that she hadn't told me anything about. I nodded, not quite sure what Charlotte was trying to tell me. Charlotte explained that she'd had to take the job as she needed to get away from a man that she had fallen in love with. I laughed, 'Why would you want to leave a man you loved?.' 'Because the man I'm in love with is already married.' Charlotte replied. Charlotte's response didn't surprise me in the slightest, she was always dating married men, but it was what she told me after that, that knocked me for six. 'I'm having an affair with Sebastian!' She told me nervously. All of a sudden, my world had come crashing down around me. Had I heard her right? Charlotte and Sebastian were having an affair. The words started to swim round in my head, after that point of the conversation. I got the gist of what had been going on. Charlotte and Sebastian had been sleeping together for over two years apparently. Sebastian had been prepared to leave me for her, but she told him that she wouldn't have been able to live with the guilt of splitting us up, or making me a one parent family. So she ended the affair and moved to America to start again. Well that had been her intention, but she just couldn't bear not being able to see Sebastian. She said that over the last seven months, she and Sebastian had been seeing each other again. All of Sebastian's so called business trips had just been an excuse for him to fly to America and see Charlotte. It was at that precise moment that it dawned on me that it was Charlotte, Sebastian had been telling that he loved, when I overheard him on the telephone at home.

No wonder she'd acted strangely when I arrived at her house to pour out my heart about the troubles Sebastian and I were having. Charlotte was the cause of all my troubles! Her words cut like a knife, not only had my husband and my best friend betrayed me, but in one fell swoop I'd lost my husband and my oldest and closest best friend. What was I going to do now? All I knew was that I needed to get out of her house, I needed time to absorb what I'd just been told. I grabbed my coat and ran out into the lane. I didn't know where I was going, it was dark and I didn't have a clue as to how I was going to get back to my hotel. I walked for about a mile in a daze, and sobbing uncontrollably. 'Could my life get any worse?' I wondered. Eventually I reached the point where I couldn't walk anymore, my feet were aching, and I was heartbroken at Charlotte and Sebastian's betrayal. All I wanted to do at that moment was sit down and die. I slumped to the ground by the side of the road and tried to pull myself together.

I saw headlights in the distance and stood up, intending to flag the car down. As the car approached, I saw that it was a taxi. I flagged the taxi down and realised that it was the taxi driver who had taken me to Jensen's house the first time I visited it. The driver asked me if I needed any help. 'Yes.' I replied before bursting into tears, whilst trying to explain where I needed to be! The driver couldn't make any sense of anything I was saying, nor where I wanted to be. Luckily he remembered taking me to Jensen's and knew where he lived. The taxi driver helped me into the cab, before setting off for Jensen's house. As we arrived at Jensen's house, Jensen came running out to the taxi to see who it was. Jensen opened the cab door and helped me from the cab. I looked at him, before collapsing in a heap on the floor. I could hear the taxi driver explaining to Jensen about how he'd found me at the side of the road, in such a state that he didn't know where I wanted to be, or what had happened to me. He explained that he remembered bringing me here, to Jensen's house before, so he thought the best thing was for him to bring me here again. Jensen thanked the taxi driver, and paid the fare, before putting his arms around me and helping me into the house.

Jensen sat me down on the sofa and asked me what had happened. He seemed concerned, and his eyes were watery in anticipation of what I was about to tell him. I managed to blurt out what Charlotte had told me, and how I'd been taken for a fool by them both! He took my face in his hands and guided my face towards his eyes so that I could see what he was about to tell me. He told me that I didn't deserve to be treated like I had been, and if there were any fools, it was them. Charlotte for betraying my friendship and Sebastian for not realising what a wonderful, loving wife I was, and that they were the losers in all of this. He told me that he couldn't understand why someone who had everything, could throw it all away. It was as though I didn't matter. Sebastian didn't deserve to be with me, and I deserved someone who would treat me with respect and love. Jensen poured me a brandy, 'To help with the shock!' he smiled, as he pulled my head to his chest and promised me that, together we would sort the mess out. 'Don't worry about anything, I'm here to help make it all better.' He reassured me, as I drifted off to sleep on the sofa. When I awoke the next day, it was late afternoon, I must have needed the sleep! I looked around the house for Jensen, to no avail, even though I could hear his voice. I peered out of the kitchen window and saw him chopping logs in the garden. I called out to him and he turned around and smiled at me. He removed his gardening gloves, threw them on top of the logs that he'd chopped, and walked across the lawn towards me. He'd been such a comfort to me last night and I just wanted to let him know that I was glad he had been there for me. He kissed me on the cheek, 'How do you feel about things today?' He asked. I took his hand and led him to the kitchen table where we sat down. I realised that he was probably wondering where he stood, with all that was going on in my life at the moment. I looked at Jensen, 'I've made a decision, I've decided to divorce Sebastian. In my heart of hearts I've known that there were problems, and that something was wrong with my marriage, for a long time. I think I just needed a little push to do something about it.' I explained. 'This whole situation has been the push I needed to put things into perspective.' I added.

I suppose I'd just plodded along for so long, what with looking after the house, and dealing with the needs of Chloe and Sebastian. I'd not given any thought to my needs. I'd concentrated on Chloe in the main, spending as much time as I could with her, seeing as she was growing up in a house filled with the atmosphere of parents who were no longer in love with each other. Don't get me wrong, Sebastian and I loved and cared deeply for Chloe, and we both showered her with love, but children aren't stupid and I knew that Chloe sensed the strained atmosphere at home.

Jensen advised me not to rush into anything, 'Just in case you regret your decision later!' He said. I told him that I'd never been as sure of anything in my life, I was divorcing Sebastian! And, as far as Charlotte was concerned, although I'd never be able to forgive her for what she had done, she had actually done me a big favour, She'd made me realise what kind of man Sebastian was! I took Jensen's hand and held it, as I told him that I wanted him to be in my life forever. I explained that, since I'd met him he'd shown me what was possible in a relationship between two people, and I couldn't go back to being starved of love and affection, as I had been with Sebastian. 'You've shown me that I can be happy. You make me feel loved, wanted, and lusted after, and that's something that I've never experienced in my marriage to Sebastian.' I told Jensen. 'Thank you for opening my eyes to all the possibilities love can offer. You've made me feel alive!' I continued, giving him a hug. 'I don't want to frighten you off, but I need to know how you feel about our relationship, and about me.' I told him. Jensen sat, silently, listening, as I spoke. I wasn't sure if that was a good thing or not, but I just needed to know where our relationship was going. Jensen looked up at me, he was crying! I put my arms around him, 'If you don't want to see me again, I'll understand.' I told him. He gave me a half smile and told me not to be silly. 'I want you to be with me forever, and I never want to lose you.' He told me. 'I thought I was going to lose you forever, I thought you were going to go back to Sebastian. I've fallen in love with you. I started to fall in love with you the night we had dinner together, back at your hotel.' He continued. The tears in his eyes and the tremble in his voice told me that he was definitely speaking from the heart. 'I love you!' He sighed, as he gazed into my eyes. 'He loves me! Wow. This sexy, caring guy in front of me loves me and it feels great.' I thought to myself, hardly believing what I'd just heard. My heart felt as though it was about to burst with happiness. I knew things wouldn't be easy for us, especially as I'd have a difficult divorce to go through! I rang my parents and told them what had gone on. They were shocked to say the least. My mother didn't believe what I was telling her, and even had the nerve to ask, 'Even if it were true, could you not forgive Sebastian's indiscretion, as he's a good provider!' I couldn't believe what I was hearing. I always knew my mother had a soft spot for Sebastian, but surely she didn't think that his behaviour was acceptable. He'd betrayed me with my best friend for over two years, it wasn't as though it was a one off fling, they'd been having a relationship! She'd annoyed me, so I told her that I wasn't able to talk to her and that I'd speak to her later on.

'Well, if you're going to ring, make it after 8 O'clock, as we're going to take Chloe to a barbeque at the Walkers.' She announced abruptly. And with that, she hung up! I put down the receiver, slightly stunned at my mother's response, and made my way back to the kitchen, a little shocked! I walked into the kitchen, where Jensen was preparing some sandwiches, and two cups of tea. 'Is everything okay?' He asked me. I nodded, but said nothing. He beckoned me to the table and I sat down. As we ate our sandwiches we got into a deep conversation about our future. After we'd finished talking I told Jensen that I wanted to go back to the hotel to get myself a change of clothes. 'How do you feel about booking out of your hotel room, and staying with me at my house?' Jensen asked. 'Yes.' I said without a hint of hesitation. 'If we're going to be together we might as well start to make plans.'

I had a quick shower and we set off to collect my things from the hotel. As we travelled back to the hotel, our conversation led to Jensen asking me how long I planned to stay in America. 'I need to go back to England at some point, but I can probably stay for another week. I've a divorce to sort out, and Sebastian and I will have to discuss where Chloe's going to live. He's bound to try to stop me bringing Chloe to live in America.' I explained to Jensen. At the hotel I asked the manager if he'd prepare my hotel bill whilst I went up to my room to pack my things. I asked if

I'd had any messages while I'd been out. I was sure that Charlotte must have spoken to Sebastian about our meeting the previous night, and thought he might have tried to get in touch, but he hadn't. It just proved to me what I'd known all along, that Sebastian only thought about himself! Jensen helped me to carry my bags from my room. I settled my bill and walked out of the hotel, with the man I loved beside me. This was to be a new beginning for both of us and I couldn't wait to grasp the future with both hands. On our way back to Jensen's, we made plans to go out and celebrate our union. Jensen wouldn't tell me where he was taking me, but I had to get dressed up as we were going somewhere special.

CHAPTER 5

That evening I wore my favourite black silk dress. It fitted me like a glove, hugging my body and showing off my womanly curves. It made me feel very, very, sexy. Jensen winked his approval when he saw me, and gave my bum a friendly pat. Jensen wore his tuxedo again, and he looked good enough to eat. Maybe that would come later! A horn 'beeped' outside and Jensen took my arm and led me outside to a waiting limousine. The chauffer escorted us to the car, and once inside, he served us a glass of champagne before taking us on our journey. Eventually, we arrived at a small restaurant in the next town. It overlooked the marina and was enchanting. We were shown to a table outside, where we were able to take in the breathtaking view. 'Fairy' lights adorned the outside walls, making it look as though the stars had come down from the sky to celebrate our union, with us. For the first time in my life I knew what it was like to be wooed. As we waited for our starters to be served, a man approached our table, playing a violin, and asked us if we had any requests. Jensen and I looked at each other, and giggled, as we couldn't think of any songs for the violinist to play. 'Okay, not to worry. I'll play something nice for you.' the violinist told us, and began to play a beautiful tune.

Jensen took my hand. I thought he was going to ask me up to dance, but he knelt down on one knee. 'I can't envisage you not being in my life now.' He said. 'Will you do me the honour of becoming my wife?' He asked. I couldn't believe my ears. 'Yes, yes.' I replied as he pulled a small box from his trouser pocket. Jensen opened the box to reveal the most beautiful ring that I'd seen in my life. It was white gold, set with my favourite stones, Tanzanite and Diamonds. Jensen took the ring from the box and placed it on my finger, to the delight of everyone in the restaurant, who applauded and cheered. Jensen stood up, leaned over the table and kissed me. 'I know you're still married and you have some issues to sort out, including your divorce, but I wanted to show you how much you mean to me. 'I want you to know how serious I am about making you, me and Chloe a family.' Here in front of me, sat a man who hadn't even met my daughter, Chloe, yet loved and cared about me so much, that he was prepared to take us into his life and home. 'What a special man you are.' I smiled to myself. As we ate our meal and drank our wine we chatted constantly, oblivious to the fact that the restaurant staff were closing up for the night. I didn't want the night to end. In the restaurant the band announced that it would be playing its last song of the night. Jensen offered his arm to me, which I took, as he led me to the dance floor and pulled me close to his body as we danced to their rendition of 'The Best of Love' by Michael Bolton. The song lyrics summed up everything that I felt towards Jensen. He really did give me the best of love, this was our song! As we swayed in time to the music, the sound of his beating heart comforted me and gave me a sense of safety and security. His body pressed against mine and set my senses racing. My body ached with passion, as he gently kissed the nape of my neck. My head began to spin and my breathing started to speed up, I was drunk on passion, and I wanted to feel like this forever. The music stopped, yet we carried on dancing, making our own music to dance to, in our heads. I could have stayed there all night had it not been for the waiters discreetly coughing, to remind us that it was time to leave.

Jensen paid the bill and led me outside to our limousine, which had pulled up at the roadside. Jensen politely opened my door and I climbed into the back of the limo. Jensen walked round to the other side of the limousine, the chauffer opened the door, and Jensen joined me in the back of the car. As we set off for Jensen's house the chauffer raised the privacy screen between the front and back seats. Jensen and I kissed so tenderly that my lips tingled and I felt as though I was floating in the sky. My whole body ached for Jensen's touch. I hadn't noticed that the car had stopped, nor that the chauffer had opened the door of the car so we could get out. I guess I got caught up in the moment. I stepped from the car, a little embarrassed at being caught in the moment. The chauffer hadn't taken us back to Jensen's house, but had pulled up at a hotel. I turned and looked at Jensen, he smiled, 'I've arranged for us to stay here for the night, I hope you don't mind!' We climbed out of the limousine and walked up the steps to the hotel entrance, where the hotel doorman opened the door, and welcomed us inside. We booked in and took the lift to the honeymoon suite. Jensen opened the door of the suite and turned to me. 'I want to make tonight a special night, one that you'll never forget.' He told me. He'd certainly done that! The room was very pretty, a vase of Lilies sat on the coffee table, alongside a bottle of Champagne, two glasses, and a box of chocolates. I liked Lilies, they had a simple elegance about them.

A sliding door separated the lounge from the bedroom. I slid open the door to reveal a king sized, four-poster bed. I explored the room a little further and found the En-suite, which was accessible through a second door from the bedroom. The En-suite boasted a Jacuzzi bath, and a shower made for two. Jensen handed me a glass of Champagne, and we toasted our new life together. I told Jensen how much I loved him, and he responded by telling me how he felt the same way. Jensen beckoned me over to him and we started to dance, just as we had in the restaurant. It didn't matter that there was no music playing, we made our own music!

His muscular arms encased my body and as he held me close, I could smell the sweet scent of his after-shave. I gently kissed his neck and playfully nibbled his ear. He began to moan with pleasure as I explored his ears with my tongue. I could feel his penis harden as it pressed against my groin and I longed for him to make love to me, but I wanted to pleasure him first. I began to unbutton his bow tie and then his shirt, to reveal his tanned, muscular chest. My tongue traced the outline of his body. His skin was soft and smooth. He pulled my head tighter to him as I licked and kissed his chest. I started to unbutton his trousers and he gasped, as my hand wandered over the tip of his erect penis. I slipped him into my mouth, and began to move slowly up and down his length, flicking my tongue around his tip with each stroke.

Jensen's penis became lubricated and he groaned once again. 'Mmm he tastes so good.' I thought to myself. Jensen pulled me to my feet, where he began to undo my dress. It slipped to the floor to reveal my black silk camisole and French knickers. My nipples stood erect and could be seen, protruding through the soft cloth of my camisole. Jensen ran his hands over my body, moving more slowly over my fully aroused breasts. The silky material brushed against my nipples, sending shivers down my spine. Jensen teased first one nipple, then the other, with his lips, before flicking each of them with his tongue. I could feel myself getting moist between the legs. Jensen's hands traced a path to my knickers, and he began to rub over the top of my knickers. The silky material rubbed against my clitoris, and I began to cum. Jensen knelt in front of me, pulled my knickers to one side, and began to drink from my wet mound. Jensen stood up and started to kiss my neck. His breath was warm against my skin and the feeling intensified my lusty desires. He cupped my face in his hands and whispered that he loved me, before gently kissing my lips. Jensen picked me up and carried me over to the bed, where he laid me down. He gently climbed on top of me, and guided his penis into my moist hole. I gasped as he began making love to me, slowly and rhythmically, awakening every sense in my body. Jensen changed the pace of his lovemaking and my body writhed in ecstasy, as Jensen and I reached orgasm together, our bodies twitching as we came. As we lay holding each other, I could feel Jensen's heart beating frantically. It was the last thing I remembered, before drifting off to sleep in each other's arms. This certainly had been a night I'd never forget, a night we'd given ourselves to each other, for life!

The following morning I awoke before Jensen. I lay with my hand on my head, watching him sleep. He looked quite cute, the way he slept. I watched his chest rise and fall with each breath, he looked so peaceful lying there, it would have been a shame to wake him so I left him sleeping while I got up and went to take a shower. As I soaped myself down, the feeling of the creamy lather on my body started to turn me on, so I let my hands explore my body. I was so immersed in the moment, and the feeling of the lather against my skin, that I hadn't noticed Jensen had come into the bathroom. He watched as

I played with, and touched myself, before joining me in the shower. He encouraged me to carry on exploring myself, his hands gliding over mine, as he stroked and caressed me. I teased myself and soon exploded in ecstasy. Jensen lifted me to waist height and leant me against the shower wall before lowering me onto his erect penis, the water splashing against our skin as we rhythmically made love. Afterwards we washed and towel dried each other. I had no idea that making love with someone you cared about could be so fulfilling. It had never been like that with Sebastian, it was more of a quick fumble, and as long as Sebastian got his sexual relief, then that was the job done, even if I hadn't had my release!

I ordered our breakfast and we sat down to plan our day. I didn't think that anything or anyone could spoil today, I was so happy. I put Sebastian to the back of my mind. I certainly wasn't going to let the thought of him and his antics ruin my day! Jensen and I decided to return to the Amish village to pick up the items of furniture that he'd bought when we'd last visited. 'I wonder what they could be, Oh well, I'll find out soon enough!' I thought. Jensen had done a good job of keeping his purchases secret, and on our way to the Amish village we called at Jensen's house to pick up his truck, so that we could collect his mystery furniture, and my quilts!

On arrival at the Amish village we were met by Mary-beth, she waved, and pointed towards the barn, where Tobias was busy sanding down a bench. He greeted us warmly and asked if we'd come to collect our furniture. Jensen nodded, and followed Tobias out of the barn. As the two of them left, Marybeth walked into the barn and offered me a glass of homemade lemonade, which I gratefully accepted. I followed her into the kitchen and was greeted with the smell of freshly baked bread. 'Would you and Jensen like to join us for lunch?' She asked. 'We'd love to!' I replied. My mouth was watering at the thought! As Marybeth and I stood talking, I could hear Jensen and Tobias talking outside. I went outside to see what they were doing. I caught sight of Jensen's truck. It was full to the brim with the furniture he'd bought, but it was covered over, so I still couldn't see what he'd bought. 'Let me see. Let me see what you've bought.' I begged. 'No! You'll have to wait until we get to our house.' He told me. 'Really?' I replied, although I quite liked the way he teased me by making me wait to see what he'd bought, and did he say, our house? Just more proof that Jensen certainly wasn't a selfish man. Marybeth called us to eat lunch. She had baked a chicken pie and there were bowls of fresh vegetables to accompany it. As usual, the kitchen table was laden from end to end, and the fresh bread that I'd smelled earlier, took pride of place in the centre of the table. We all tucked into the hearty feast, and thanked our hosts for their kindness when we'd finished eating. I enjoyed visiting the village, a sense of calm filled the air, and made me feel very relaxed. The village, and those living in it, seemed to bring out the inner peace in people, and that was a very nice feeling. On our way back to Jensen's house, we chatted about the night before. Our night of magical lovemaking! Jensen told me that he never expected to fall in love again after having his heart broken, by his ex-fiancé back in England. 'You've made me the happiest person alive. I'm a very lucky man!' He told me. 'I was the lucky one.' I thought.

Back at the house, Jensen began unloading his furniture. 'Close your eyes, whilst I get it all off the truck.' He told me. I shut my eyes as he'd asked but I really wanted to peep. I guess it was my inner child coming through. Jensen seemed to draw feelings and emotions from me that I'd long since forgotten that I'd had! I heard Jensen close the back of the truck up. Finally, Jensen said, 'Now open your eyes!' I opened my eyes, and there before me stood the most beautifully carved bed frame, and a rocking chair, made for a small child. I looked at, and touched the bed frame. It was so smooth. I did the same to the rocking chair, and on further inspection I saw that Chloe's name had been carved into the wooden, chair back. I flung my arms around Jensen's neck and gave him a big kiss. 'Oh thank you Jensen, they're beautiful.' I told him, as tears ran down my face. As he wiped away my tears, Jensen said, 'Out with the old and in with the new, the bed is our new bed,' He explained. 'A fresh start in a new relationship!' He added. How thoughtful he was, I was taken aback at his present for Chloe, bearing in mind he'd never even met her. I felt that Jensen was showing me, in his own way, that he was prepared to treat Chloe as his own. Jensen was such a wonderful man. I had to keep pinching myself to make sure I wasn't dreaming.

I helped Jensen carry our new bed, and Chloe's rocking chair into the house. We moved the old wrought iron bedstead into the spare bedroom, and I looked at Jensen and laughed. 'What you laughing at?' He asked. 'We've forgotten to perform the most important task.' I told him. 'We haven't christened the new bed!' I continued, with a twinkle in my eye. I threw a pillow towards Jensen, who proceeded to chase me round the bed. Eventually I allowed Jensen to catch me, and we both fell onto the new bed. Jensen took me in his arms and showered my body with kisses. We frantically tore at each other's clothing, unable to contain our sexual urges. I pushed Jensen onto his back and jumped on top of him. I grabbed hold of his manhood, and shoved it inside me, before frantically riding him to orgasm. This had been a rampant, wanton, lovemaking session, a quickie. Only a quickie could have satisfied and fulfilled our desires. Sometimes, when the moment gets you, as it just had us, it didn't matter that it wasn't slow and tender, as it usually was. Lust had taken hold of us and we'd just followed our carnal desires and urges. Very satisfying!

We got up and adjusted our clothing. Jensen winked at me and told me that I was leading him astray. I laughed and replied that he shouldn't have made room in his wardrobe for my clothes if he didn't want to be corrupted. Jensen promised to make me my own wardrobe, once I'd moved in properly. Jensen was good with his hands in more ways than one. I was turning into a raving nymphomaniac. I'd gone from one extreme to the other. With Sebastian, lovemaking had been such a chore, and not a very fulfilling one either! With Jensen, lovemaking was a totally opposite experience. I'd become more adventurous and daring, Jensen and I had explored one another's bodies in ways I could never have imagined possible. I found myself using my imagination for the first time in years. I did to Jensen what I thought he would enjoy. Letting his responses guide me when I used my hands, and other parts of my body on him! The way we touched each other and the way we made love to each other always seemed so natural, and everything fell into place, it was so perfect.

The Sun was shining brightly outside, it was such a lovely day and too good to waste. We decided that we'd go on a picnic. 'I'd like you to meet some of my friends.' He told me. I was a bit nervous at the thought, especially as I didn't know how much they knew about me. Did they know that I was still married to someone else? Jensen assured me everything would be fine. 'They'll love you as much as I do.' Jensen replied, sensing my nervousness. Jensen phoned a few of his friends and arranged for us to meet them at a nearby lake for a picnic. We filled a picnic hamper with crusty bread, various cheeses, fruit, wine and a selection of salad vegetables.

I changed into a sundress that I'd brought with me. I didn't want to be overdressed, but at the same time I didn't want to look like a tramp. It had been quite a few years since I'd met anybody's friends for the first time. I suppose I was a little out of practice, but I felt it was important for me to make a good impression and get on with Jensen's friends, after all I intended to be in Jensen's life for the foreseeable future. We loaded up Jensen's truck and set off for the lake. Jensen told me that it would take about an hour to reach the lake, so I sat back and enjoyed the beautiful scenery as we travelled up to the lake. When we arrived, a few of Jensen's friends were already there. Jensen acknowledged them as he pulled onto the grassy area next to the lake. We climbed out of the truck's cab and Jensen introduced me to his friends, 'Arabella, this is Jake, this is Melissa, and those two are Toby and Heather.' He told me, pointing to his friends. 'Hello, Arabella.' They all replied. They all seemed very friendly. 'It's nice to finally meet the person who's been keeping Jensen so busy lately.' Jake declared, with a wry smile. I blushed, and wondered what Jensen had been telling them about me.

I think Jensen could tell that I was beginning to feel a little out of my depth. He put his arm around my waist to reassure me. I found Jensen very thoughtful like that. As young as Jensen was, he was surprisingly mature, and he suitably impressed me. Heather called me over, 'Do you fancy playing volleyball with us?' She asked. 'Yes. I'd love to.' I nodded, and followed Heather down to the lakeside where they were playing. I hadn't played volleyball in years, but I was looking forward to having a go. It was nice to be able to take time out from all the usual day to day drudgery, and the beck and call of someone. Just to have fun and concentrate on being myself. I wasn't very good, but everyone made me feel at ease. I couldn't believe that I had been worrying unnecessarily about meeting Jensen's friends, they were all really nice.

After about an hour, we sat down to our picnic. The others had also brought along a selection of food, and once everything was laid out on the picnic rug, it looked an impressive spread. We all tucked in, and after we'd all overindulged, we lay on the freshly mown grass to recover from eating so much. Jensen took off his shirt and gave it to me to use as a pillow. I put his shirt under my head, while Jensen lay on the ground next to me. He kissed my nose and brushed my hair from my face, this was bliss. I gazed into his sexy, green eyes and mouthed 'I love you.' He gave me a smile and mouthed that he loved me too. I couldn't take my eyes off him. I scanned Jensen's masculine physique, and studied his facial features. 'My god, you're handsome!' I thought to myself. I could quite easily have fallen into his deep, and beautiful green eyes, and when he looked at me, he made me melt. I looked at Jensen's lips. They were thin and sensuous and he certainly made my body quiver when he pressed them against my body. I took Jensen's hands and playfully nibbled and sucked each of his fingers in turn. I could see that I was beginning to turn him on, as the bulge in his trousers started to grow! Jensen pulled himself closer to me and started to kiss me, so gently. His lips were so soft, and when he put them against mine, my body reacted to his touch. My nipples ached, and were visibly erect through my flimsy sundress. 'Go and get a room!' Jake shouted, then burst into laughter. Jensen and I looked at each other and giggled. We couldn't help it, we just enjoyed touching each other.

The Sun beat down on us as we lay in one another's arms, enjoying the day. I could hear the birds singing in the trees, and the stream, that ran into the lake, rushing by. It was certainly a magical place, and very serene. Over by the lake, Toby and Melissa were splashing each other with water, and before long they turned their attention to Jensen and I, and began splashing us. Jensen stood up, ran down to the lake, jumped into the water with his clothes on, and joined in. they all shouted for me to join them, although I wasn't wearing a swimsuit, I didn't care, nor did it matter. I just went along with the feel of the moment, ran towards the lake and jumped, fully clothed into the water. 'Ooh, it's cold.' I gasped, as we splashed about like a bunch of teenagers. It was the most fun I'd had in ages. We all climbed out of the lake, wet through, and lay down on the grass to dry off. We all spent the next couple of hours drying out, before calling it a day. We said our 'goodbyes', promising to meet up again at a later date. I'd had a brilliant day. As we drove back to Jensen's house, he thanked me for meeting his friends. 'They've all remarked on how nice you are.' Jensen told me. 'They told me how they'd been watching how you looked at me, and how obvious it was that you are in love with me.' I thought that was such a lovely thing for them to say. I guess I'd just been given their seal of approval, and that made me feel good, and accepted.

As we approached the outskirts of town, Jensen stopped off at the local store to pick up some supplies. When he returned to the truck, Jensen's face carried a beaming smile. I was getting to know Jensen's smiles, and this latest smile meant that he was up to something! We arrived at Jensen's house and he headed into the kitchen, while I went and sat on the back veranda. He put everything that he'd bought away, with the exception of one item that he was hiding behind his back! 'Here you are, Arabella. I've bought you a little something.' And he handed me a CD. It was The Very Best of Michael Bolton, I've bought you it because it's got our song, The Best of Love, on it. Jensen put on the CD and we started to dance. We pressed up against each other, and held on to each other throughout the whole CD, just enjoying the moment, and the closeness we shared. I felt a million dollars. I'd never had as much attention paid to me, ever, and it wasn't strained or forced, it was natural and I liked the feeling! I liked the feeling a lot! If this was an indication of what lay ahead of me for the rest of my life, then I would die a very happy and contented woman, a woman with no regrets. I've always believed in fate, and Jensen was my fate.

All the upset I'd gone through, with Sebastian and Charlotte, made me realise that I hadn't been living my life, just existing. How are you able to know when you've found love, if you've not experienced pain? With Sebastian, I was just going through the motions, there was no feeling of love, just numbness and emptiness. It was a bit like that old, comfy cardigan that you don't want to discard, even though you've outgrown it, for fear of the unknown. I suppose the saying, better the devil you know was quite appropriate where my relationship with Sebastian was concerned. Yet with Jensen everything was so different. He wasn't frightened of showing his emotions, of sharing his love, of enjoying our bodies. The sadness was, that for years I had denied myself the chance to share in all those wonderful things. Things were going to change from now on. I wasn't going to be frightened of moving forwards and I would embrace change, because change was good! Jensen explained that he had to work the next few days, so I had time to myself, to do as I pleased. I didn't like the thought of being away from Jensen for hours on end. I suppose he'd spoilt me by giving all of himself to me for the last few weeks, I'd got used to having him all to myself! I knew I was being selfish but I couldn't help it. We snuggled up together on the sofa for the rest of the night, and there we stayed until the following morning.

Jensen woke early. He made me a cup of coffee and a plate of pancakes and woke me with them just as he was on his way to work. I tucked in to my pancakes, enjoying every mouthful before finishing off with my cup of coffee. I liked being spoilt and looked after! I decided to get up and take a shower, before taking a walk into the nearby town. Just as I was getting up, my mobile rang, it was Charlotte calling so I rejected the call. 'What a bloody cheek.' I muttered. Charlotte was the last person I wanted to speak to. I freshened up in the shower, and slipped into a pair of jeans. It had turned a bit chilly outside, so I borrowed one of Jensen's jumpers. It had his scent on it. 'Mmm. Lovely.' I said to myself. I liked Jensen's scent.

I picked up my bag and phone, there had been four missed calls from Charlotte. 'Well she's certainly eager to get in touch all of a sudden.' I thought. I couldn't be doing with speaking to her at the moment so I turned off my phone. The walk to town was very pleasant. America certainly boasted some lovely countryside. I'd always imagined America as a skyscraper ridden, overbuilt country, well that was what it looked like on TV! I suppose I thought everywhere in America looked like New York, but here in New England the countryside was simply breathtaking. I thought I'd cook something special for Jensen tonight, after all he'd done a splendid job of looking after me so far, and I wanted to return the compliment.

I bought some beef, flour, and suet as I was going to cook Jensen good, old-fashioned, stew and dumplings. I purchased some organic vegetables from the local greengrocer, to go into the stew, and decided that I'd finish the meal off with a homemade Banoffee pie. Back home in England that was one of my signature dishes amongst my friends. I spotted a beautiful angel necklace in a shop window, so I entered the shop as I've always had a love of anything to do with angels, whether it be ornaments, pictures or jewellery. The sales assistant showed me the necklace, she said it was a unisex necklace, and that for a man, it came on a thicker gold chain. I bought one for Jensen, and had the sales assistant engrave a message on the back. It read, 'Two Hearts United Forever'. I hoped Jensen liked it. I finished my shopping and walked back to the house. I was busy cooking for the rest of the afternoon, and didn't hear Jensen walk through the door. I told him to sit on the sofa whilst I got him a drink. I poured him a whisky and coke and took it to him in the lounge.

The food wasn't due to be ready for at least forty minutes, so while Jensen relaxed with his drink, I ran him a bath. Once Jensen's bath was run, I called to him. Jensen came into the bathroom, got undressed, and climbed into the bath. I began to wash his shoulders and back. 'I could get quite used to this!' Jensen declared. 'I hope you do! I enjoy pampering you, especially when you've been working hard all day.' I replied, my hands gliding over him, and soaping the various parts of his body, if you know what I mean, lingering longer in some places longer than others! The timer on the cooker bleeped, telling me that the food was cooked, and ready to be served.

I handed Jensen a towel, and left him in the bathroom to finish getting dried, while I went into the kitchen to serve up dinner. A couple of minutes later, Jensen walked into the kitchen, wearing some cut-off denim shorts, and a tee-shirt. 'Wow!' I thought, 'I'll have some of that!' I served Jensen his food, and he tucked into it. I liked a man who enjoyed his food. Even the way Jensen ate was sexy! 'God, what's wrong with me? I seem to be permanently aroused just lately.' I thought to myself, I wasn't complaining though! 'Would you mind if I don't have my pudding until later? I've no room to fit it in.' said Jensen, patting his stomach. I told him that was okay. Jensen stood up and told me that I deserved a reward for making such a lovely meal, and asked me to follow him, which I did. He led me into the bedroom and asked me to get undress and lie, face down on the bed. 'I'm going to give you a massage.' He explained. I quite fancied a massage. I used to go for one once a week, at my local beauty salon back home. I was looking forward to this!

Jensen picked up a bottle of baby oil and poured some into his hands, before pouring a little onto my back. His hands glided over my skin, kneading and pressing softly, all over my back. I sighed with pleasure as he massaged the small of my back, and with long, sweeping strokes he massaged all my woes away. Jensen then rubbed oil on my bum, and with gentle, fingertip strokes, he massaged my skin. That was quite a sensuous experience. I'd never had my bum massaged before, but I'd certainly let Jensen massage it again! Jensen carried on massaging me, working his way down each of my legs to my feet. Then he took each of my toes in turn and gently sucked at them. Jensen had full control of my body. I was on fire, in a sexual sense, and I shivered in anticipation of what he might do next. Jensen told me to turn onto my back, so I did as he asked as I couldn't wait for him to explore more of me! He began massaging my feet before working his way up the front of my legs, and on to my stomach. He made circular movements on my skin with his fingers, then he began kissing around my navel, his hot breath reacting with my skin, making my body tingle with desire. He carried on kissing me, softly, across my stomach and then across the top of my pubic hair. I wanted to take his head in my hands and guide his mouth to my throbbing vagina. I longed for him to taste and probe me with his tongue, but he moved his hands up my body, towards my aroused breasts, where my nipples sat proudly erect waiting for his touch. He gently squeezed and massaged my breasts, before rubbing more oil onto them. His hands circled and cupped them, he teased my nipples with his tongue and took them in his mouth. I was at boiling point with passion as his lips moved to my mouth. He kissed me passionately, his lips pressing hard against mine, his tongue exploring my mouth. I gasped with pleasure as he removed his clothes. All the while his lips remained pressed hard against my lips. He lay his body on top of mine, his erect penis pushing against my groin before it found its way into my throbbing, hot, wet pussy. Jensen began to slowly push in and out of my love hole, until I came all over him. He moaned and groaned, as he too, climaxed. We lay holding each other for a while, then I told him that I'd bought him a present, and got up to go and fetch it from the kitchen. I came back into the bedroom, clutching the box containing the necklace. I told him that I wanted to give him something to always remind him of my love for him.

He opened the box and took out the chain. He read the inscription on the back and looked up at me. His eyes were watering, and his lips quivered with emotion. 'That's the nicest present anyone has ever bought me. I'll treasure it forever!' He declared. I placed the chain around his neck, and fastened it. We hugged and Jensen took my hands and kissed my fingers. 'You mean the world to me Arabella, and I'm never gonna let you go. You're stuck with me forever!' That suited me just fine. I took Jensen's hand and led him into the kitchen. We sat down at the table and I spoon-fed him some of the Banoffee pie I'd made. Jensen returned the favour by feeding me!

We talked about our day and I mentioned that Charlotte had rung, several times. I told Jensen that I couldn't face talking to her so I had switched my phone off. 'Aren't you just a little bit curious about what she wanted?' He enquired. 'No I'm not! I'm not interested in anything she has to say. As far as I'm concerned, Charlotte doesn't exist.' I replied, matter of factly. 'Go and turn your phone on, she might have left you a message about the reason she rang.' He suggested. Curiosity got the better of me, so I took my phone out of my bag and switched it on. I'd had three more calls from Charlotte and, rather surprisingly, one from Sebastian, who'd left a message asking me to contact him, urgently! 'Yeah, right!' I thought. I had no intention of ringing Sebastian. He was probably just ringing to see what my plans were, since I'd found out about his affair with Charlotte. 'Well, you can stew!' I said out loud. Jensen looked across at me and smiled. 'Sounds like you need some fresh air. Let's walk to the bar in town, it's only fifteen minutes from here.' He said. 'Good idea.' I replied. I grabbed Jensen's hand and pulled him from his chair. 'Come on, let's go!' I told him.

We took a leisurely stroll into town and arrived at the bar. The locals all stared at us as we walked into the bar, then we heard someone call Jensen's name. It was Jake. He was in the bar with Toby, they beckoned us over, and invited us to join them. Toby and Jake were both surprised to see Jensen, as he was usually at home in the evening, busying himself with his carpentry, and making things for his home. 'You're a good influence on Jensen.' They told me. 'It's good to see him getting out of the house a bit more.' Jensen ordered a round of drinks, and we spent the rest of the evening chatting with Jake and Toby. I'd really enjoyed myself and, in all honesty, I was a little tipsy. I was pleased that Jake had offered to give us a lift home. As we walked outside, to Jake's car, the crisp air filled my lungs and made me a bit unsteady on my feet. Back at home, Jensen carried me from the car and into the house. Jensen carried me into the bedroom. I bet he was glad that his house was all on one level, I couldn't imagine him relishing the thought of carrying me up a flight of stairs! Jensen placed me on the bed and undressed me, before covering me with a quilt, and climbing into bed beside me, where we remained until morning!

CHAPTER 6

I woke to the sound of my mobile ringing. I looked at the clock, it was only six–thirty in the morning. 'Who could possibly be ringing at this time?' I wondered. I picked up my phone to see who'd called, the screen showed that it was Sebastian ringing. 'You'd better answer it.' Said Jensen, 'It might be important, especially with him ringing this early in the morning!' Reluctantly, I answered my phone. 'Hello! What do you want? Do you know what time it is?' I angrily enquired. 'Where are you, we've been trying to get hold of you!' Sebastian replied. 'Who's 'We' I asked, 'You mean you and Charlotte?' I snapped back at him. 'Look, I haven't rung to argue with you, I'm ringing to tell you that Chloe's in hospital. She's had an accident.' Sebastian explained. 'Oh my god, is she alright?' I screamed. 'What happened?' Sebastian explained that Chloe had fallen into the Walker's pond whilst she'd been at a barbecue there with my mum and dad. Sebastian told me that Chloe had been rushed to hospital and was in a coma! My head was spinning. I couldn't breathe. My daughter was in a coma! Sebastian told me that the nurses weren't sure if she would pull through. I was struggling to comprehend what Sebastian was telling me. In shock, I spluttered something about booking myself on the first flight back to England, and told him I'd ring him once I'd sorted something out.

I put down my mobile, and leapt out of bed. Jensen asked me what was wrong. I explained what had been said, and that I needed to get back to England as soon as possible. Jensen told me to get ready, and he would sort out the flight for me. 'Do you want me to come to England with you?' Jensen asked. It was nice that Jensen had offered to come to England with me, and offering me moral support, but I felt that it was something I needed to do myself. 'The next available flight to England is due to depart at ten o clock this morning.' Jensen told me. I packed my things, and Jensen loaded them into his truck so that we were ready to go. I looked at the kitchen clock, it was seven–thirty. I didn't know what to do with myself. The time seemed to be dragging. I just wanted to get on the plane, so I could see my Chloe. I rang Sebastian, he agreed to meet me off the plane and take me to the hospital. Jensen insisted that I sat down and ate something. 'You must eat, you need to be fit and strong for Chloe.' He said.

'Not eating will only make you sick.' He added. He was right. I was pleased Jensen had taken charge, I was running around like a headless chicken. I needed Jensen to help me through this and he'd certainly stepped up to the mark. Jensen brought me my bacon and eggs, and a pot of strong coffee. I had to admit, I did feel a little stronger now that I'd eaten something. We set off for the airport in plenty of time for me to collect my ticket. Jensen carried my suitcase into the terminal, and found out what gate my flight was leaving from. Jensen had been unusually quiet, throughout the drive to the airport, and I asked him why. 'Don't worry about me, just concentrate on Chloe.' He told me. I refused to let the subject drop though, and persistence finally paid off, as Jensen explained that he was worried that I wouldn't return to America and him. 'You don't have to worry about that.' 'You've made me the happiest I've been in a long time, and I love you.'

I told him that I couldn't comprehend a life without him being in it, and I was definitely coming back to him! Coming back to him and the new beginning that we had promised to ourselves. I just had to sort things out in England first. I needed to help Chloe recover, sort out with Sebastian, where Chloe was going to live, and commence divorce proceedings. I wasn't sure how long all of it would take, but I knew that I'd be returning to America, and Jensen whatever the outcome.

The terminal address system announced my flight, and Jensen put his arms around me and kissed me. He told me to be strong, as everything would work out fine. His voice was shaking with emotion, and I could see from the tears in his eyes, and the look on his face that he was hurting. We both cried and held onto each other, not wanting to let go of one another. The last call for my flight was called, so we walked towards the boarding desk, our hands tightly entwined. At the desk, Jensen kissed me again and said that he would ring me every day. With Jensen's last words going round in my head, I got on the plane, not daring to look back towards Jensen, and his breaking heart. My flight back to England was just a blur. I spent most of it sleeping. We finally touched down in London and I made my way through the airport terminal, towards the exit. As arranged, Sebastian was waiting for me. He leaned forward to kiss me, but I pulled away, and we walked to the car in silence and made our way to the hospital.

We arrived at the hospital a short while later, and Sebastian dropped me off at the hospital's entrance and sped off out of the exit gates. I guess he wasn't going to come in and see Chloe then. I made my way to the ward that Chloe was on and informed the nurse at the desk that I was Chloe's mum. The nurse asked me to follow her, and she took me to Chloe's room. Chloe had been put in a room by herself and I was glad that they had as nothing could have prepared me for the shock as I entered the room. As I walked up to Chloe's bedside, all I could see were tubes, monitors and machinery, and amongst all of it lay Chloe. I choked back my tears as I saw my little girl laid on the bed, so helpless, with a ventilator coming from her mouth. I swallowed hard and tried to hold back the tears but it was no good, and I sobbed as I rushed to hold Chloe's hand. The nurse who was responsible for looking after Chloe, explained that it could be quite daunting for loved ones to see all the equipment surrounding someone close to them. She wasn't wrong. She carried on explaining that the equipment was there to help Chloe, and to keep reminding myself of that. The nurse encouraged me to keep talking to Chloe, as people who have been in coma's before have regained consciousness, and have spoken of the various conversations they've heard whilst in a comatose state.

The nurse said that talking to Chloe, might trigger something in Chloe's brain, to help awaken her. Taking on board what the nurse told me, I sat by Chloe's bedside for three days. Chatting about all the things she loved to do, and all the places we'd visited together, but still she slept. To see Chloe, you would think that there was nothing wrong with her. She was just in a deep sleep. I barely left Chloe's side, not even to eat or sleep, just in case I missed something.

I wanted to be there in case I missed her waking up and calling out for me. Doctors and nurses were constantly in and out of Chloe's room, carrying out various tests and checking the machines. They were testing her responses, but still Chloe slept. I told them that Chloe would wake up, it's just that she hadn't had enough sleep yet, and when she had, she would open her eyes and start chatting away as she always did. Sebastian was in and out of the hospital, checking on Chloe's progress and constantly telling me that we should talk about his affair with Charlotte. I told him that I didn't want to talk to him about any of it, I just wanted to concentrate on getting Chloe better. Nothing else mattered at the moment, Chloe's condition was the most important thing to sort out, everything else could be sorted out later. Anyway, I wasn't going to ease his guilty conscience.

Over the following few days, the doctors continued to monitor Chloe's condition. They approached Sebastian and I about the possibility that Chloe may never wake up and recover. They were words that I didn't want to hear, Chloe would wake up, she just had too! As promised, Jensen kept phoning me to get daily updates on Chloe's progress. He seemed genuinely more concerned than Sebastian, her own father was! Over the days that followed, Sebastian's visits to the hospital had dwindled. His excuse was that he was busy at work. But deep down, I think he had given up hope that Chloe was going to recover. This was about the same time as the doctor had advised us to prepare for the possibility of Chloe not regaining consciousness. A month had passed, and there were still no signs of improvement in Chloe's condition. She just carried on sleeping. I was virtually living at the hospital by her bedside, I'd only called at my house once since returning to England. There were no reasons to be there, Sebastian's visits to the hospital, to see Chloe, had ceased completely. 'He's given up on her' I thought. Well I certainly hadn't, nor would I!

Over time I'd become friendly with some of the nurses who worked on Chloe's ward. They would often bring me a cuppa and a sandwich, and sometimes they stayed and chatted with me as I sat by Chloe's bed, stroking her hair and talking to her. I'd stopped going to the hospital canteen, as I'd see people giving me a sympathetic look, that look people gave you when they think that you are fighting a losing battle, but just won't come to terms with the fact. Chloe wasn't a losing battle in my eyes, she was my daughter, she was precious and I refused to give up on her like some had. Time went by, with still no change. A nurse came to see me and told me that the consultant wanted to see Sebastian and I. I had to get hold of Sebastian and persuade him to come to the hospital, which he reluctantly agreed to. A few hours later, we were sat in Chloe's consultants office. One of the nurses said that the consultant would be in shortly. Eventually he arrived and set about explaining that he wanted to carry out further tests on Chloe, he wanted to take her off the ventilator to see if she could breathe on her own. I ran from the office, weeping uncontrollably. I rang Jensen and blurted my heart out to him. 'I'm not giving up on her, I'm not' I cried. I was ushered back to the consultant's office by the nurse. Sebastian and the consultant were waiting for me. The consultant explained that, by doing the tests, it would give him a good indication of where we went from there. I couldn't give my consent there and then, I needed time to think things through. I couldn't, nor wouldn't be rushed into making that decision. I was frightened of the outcome of the tests. 'What if she didn't breathe on her own? Would they just turn the machine off, and that would be that? At least if we gave Chloe more time to wake up, helped her to breathe until she did awaken….I would have some hope.' I thought.

'I wish Jensen was here, he would know what to do, he would take charge and sort it all out. He was good at that. He made me feel safe!' I thought. I composed myself and returned to the ward. A nurse had been sat talking to Chloe, and as I entered the room, she got up 'Thank you.' I said. I was thankful to her, she had taken time to sit and talk to Chloe, in case she responded. And the nurse gave me strength to carry on. I sat in the chair and noticed that someone had left a storybook for Chloe. It was the story of a princess who fell into a deep sleep for a hundred years. I began to read the story out loud to Chloe, she was my little sleeping princess. Perhaps she would wake up like the princess in the story. After a while I drifted off to sleep, with my head leant on Chloe's bed. The following morning I awoke to the sound of someone calling my name. It was Jensen! He'd taken a late flight, after speaking to me on the phone the previous day, and had just arrived in London. I leapt up and flung my arms around him. 'Oh, thank you, thank you for coming!' I said with tears streaming down my face. He told me that he couldn't let me go through this on my own, and anyway, he'd missed me like crazy! I introduced Jensen to Chloe, and Chloe to him.

I told her all about him and how he had flown thousands of miles, especially to meet her. I hoped Chloe would hear me and wake up to meet this wonderful man, who'd cared for us both so much, but she didn't and carried on sleeping. The nurses showed Jensen to a nearby bathroom, so he could freshen up after his long flight. One of the nurses came into the room and suggested that I take a break. 'I'll ring you if there's any change' she told me. I didn't want to leave Chloe's side. 'You've spent the last six weeks at Chloe's bedside, you deserve some time to get a good night's sleep and a decent meal inside you. You owe it to yourself and to Chloe, to be strong and refreshed for when she wakes up. And your man looks like he could do with some sleep too!' She added. In the end I reluctantly agreed, and Jensen and I booked into a nearby hotel. We ordered room service and both took a shower while we waited for the food to be delivered to our room. It was nice to feel Jensen's body next to mine. Not in a sexual way, we were both too tired for that, and I had more important things on my mind. We washed each other down, cleaning and washing away all our tensions. I must admit that it had been nice, being able to take a shower and wash my hair. Although I got a daily wash at the hospital, it wasn't the same as being able to get really clean as you could in a shower. We donned fluffy bathrobes that the hotel provided, and sat on the bed waiting for our food to arrive.

Eventually, one of the hotel porters knocked on the door, with our tray of steak and salad and two steaming mugs of hot chocolate. We wolfed down our food and climbed into bed. Jensen wrapped his arms tightly around me and we kissed. Our bodies were too exhausted to go any further, and as he held me close to him, I drifted off to sleep. I was glad Jensen was here with me, it meant the world to me. It's surprising how lonely and isolated you feel, spending day after day at the hospital. I didn't regret for one minute the time I'd been spending at Chloe's bedside, I just missed interacting with people. I knew that with Jensen by my side, I could cope with anything. We awoke to the sound of my alarm on my mobile going off. I'd set it to wake us up at seven o clock in the morning. We dressed and went down for breakfast. As we made our way through the breakfast buffet, Jensen kept putting food onto my plate as we passed through the different sections. He told me that I needed to keep my strength up. After breakfast we called at the hotel reception, to book in for a few more nights, before setting off to the hospital to see Chloe. For the next week, Jensen and I spent our days at the hospital at Chloe's bedside till 9pm, and the nights at the hotel. There was still no sign of Sebastian. He hadn't even bothered to visit Chloe. I think he had just given up on her and moved on with his life. Jensen had spent more time at Chloe's bedside than her own father had!

One day, whilst visiting Chloe, the nurse told me that the consultant had wanted to see me, whilst he was on his rounds. We waited in anticipation, for the consultant to arrive. When he finally arrived, he said that he had been talking to Sebastian, earlier that morning and discussed with him his concerns about the lack of improvement in Chloe's condition. They had done some more tests, on Sebastian's authorisation, and concluded that, there wasn't a shadow of doubt that Chloe would ever wake up from her coma. She was clinically brain dead, and he could see no point in keeping Chloe on the ventilator, as it wouldn't make any difference to the outcome. He also went on to say that, Sebastian had agreed with him and had given his consent for the ventilator to be switched off. I couldn't believe my ears! 'No!' I pleaded, 'Please give me more time.' But the decision had been made, the consent had been given by Sebastian, he'd gone behind my back! 'Will Sebastian be here, when you turn the ventilator off?' Jensen asked. 'No he won't, I'm afraid, he's informed me that he's too busy at work to attend.' The consultant replied. 'Huh! Sebastian's given his consent to let Chloe go, but he can't even be bothered to be here for her, in her final moments, when she'll slip away from us forever.' I cried.

'He's a selfish bastard!' I screamed, before bursting into floods of tears in Jensen's arms. After composing myself a little, Jensen and I sat on Chloe's bed, both of us holding her little hands. One by one, the machines were turned off. It took a few minutes for Chloe to slip away peacefully. 'Bye, bye, princess.' I mouthed choking back the tears......my beautiful daughter had gone! Jensen and I sat in Chloe's room, a further ten minutes or so. I sat surveying my home of the last five weeks or so, I was still holding Chloe's hand. Some of the nurses came in and offered their condolences. One of them presented me with a bag, full of Chloe's things. I expected to break down again, but I was so numb with shock. Jensen and I left Chloe's bedside, for the last time, and that was that! In a blink of an eye, I had lost one of the most precious things in my life! Jensen took me back to our hotel room. 'I'll have to ring people and let them know that Chloe's gone.' I told him. I picked up my mobile phone and rang my parents to give them the sad news. Then I let my friends know, and finally I called Sebastian. I was in too much of a shock, to have a go at him. He said that we should meet, to make the arrangements for Chloe's funeral. I agreed to go to my house later that day. I had something to do before that meeting!

I called one of my parents oldest friends, who I'd grown up around as a child. We used to call him Uncle Timothy, even though he wasn't really our uncle. He was a high flying lawyer, with a mean reputation. He would certainly give Sebastian a run for his money. Timothy agreed to see me in an hour's time. I freshened up and changed my clothes in readiness for my meeting. Jensen asked if I wanted him to come with me, but I told him that I wanted to tie up the loose ends on my own. Sebastian had shocked me to the core, when he had given his permission for Chloe's ventilator to be switched off without any discussion with me, and he couldn't even be bothered to be at Chloe's bedside as she took her last breath. Now It's payback time! I'm no longer letting myself be dictated too, by him. I arrived at Uncle Timothy's a few minutes early. His secretary showed me into his office, where he was sat behind a large oak desk. He stood up and gave me a hug and expressed his sadness at Chloe's death. I thanked him for his kind words and asked him if he could do me a huge favour.

I explained that I wanted him to draw up my divorce papers to Sebastian, straight away. As I needed to give them to him, later that day. I went against Uncle Timothy's advice 'To screw him for everything he had,' I told him that I had no interest in the house, or any of the expensive furniture that we owned, if he agreed on a quick uncontested divorce, then all I wanted was half a million pounds as a settlement figure. Sebastian was worth at least eight million, so the pittance that I wanted, would be like loose change to him. Uncle Timothy said I was mad not to demand more, but I knew what I was doing. I didn't want to get into a long drawn out battle with Sebastian, not because I was afraid to, but I just wanted him out of my life as soon as possible. I left Uncle Timothy's with the divorce papers in my hands. When I arrived at the place I used to call home, the nanny opened the door to me and I stepped inside. She told me that Sebastian wasn't at home yet, so I went upstairs to my old bedroom. I looked round the room, there wasn't one thing in the room that I had missed. This had always been a place that I retreated to, when things got tough. But I couldn't imagine why I loved spending time in this room now. I gathered all my clothes and packed them into two suitcases. I also put my photo album in my case, as it held lots of photographs of Chloe and me.

That done, I went into Chloe's bedroom to collect some of her things, one's that had the most sentimental value. I packed Chloe's favourite CD, and her favourite teddy bear. Chloe had loved her bedroom. It was all pink, and she had a giant rocking horse and dolls house. She would spend absolutely hours playing with her dolls house. I used to stand at her bedroom door sometimes, and listen to her playing happy families with her dolls. I wasn't sure what else I should pack, to take with me to America. I couldn't exactly pack all of her belongings and transport them to America, much as I would have liked too. Instead, I packed the things that I knew were her favourite things. Our nanny called to me that Sebastian had just arrived home. So I collected my suitcases and made my way downstairs, to Sebastian's study. It was rather ironic that this was where it had all started. The place where I had overheard Sebastian's conversation to Charlotte. I seemed to have gone full circle. Sebastian walked into the room and sat behind his desk, as if I was just another one of his clients.

He told me that he wanted to explain to me about him and Charlotte, but I told him that I wasn't interested in hearing his pathetic excuses. I was here solely to make arrangements for Chloe's funeral. It was agreed that Chloe would be cremated, and that her favourite song would be played at the service. We agreed that the service would be held in our local village church, in three days time. Sebastian had, apparently, already been in touch with the vicar to make the arrangements, which meant that the whole process was hastened, and we wouldn't have to wait the usual time of a week. 'Will you be coming back to stay at the house?' Sebastian enquired. 'No, I'll be staying at a hotel.' I replied. 'The house has a very cold feel about it now, and I no longer have a reason, or the desire to stay here.' I continued.

Sebastian seemed a little shocked at my reply, and quickly moved on to ask me what we were going to do about our separation. Trying to take control as usual, he offered to have some papers drawn up, offering 'Something agreeable to both of us.' which I declined with a smile, before throwing my, already drawn up divorce papers, onto his desk. Sebastian almost fell of his chair, in surprise at my forethought, he'd always been the one to make the decisions, regarding finances etc. and it gave me great pleasure to see that I'd shocked him. I'd ruffled his feathers, and he wasn't comfortable with that. The old Arabella wouldn't have dared take him on. It was in that instant that, I think he realised that I was a lot stronger than before, a lot more assertive, and that I meant business! 'I need time to think, to consider everything.' He stammered. What he really meant, was that he needed time to weigh up the damage to his pride! I generously gave him all of five minutes to consider his position, explaining that my offer was a 'once only offer' and if he didn't agree to it, then I would fight for the whole lot, everything. The house, furniture and half of his acquired wealth. How I wished that I'd had a camera with me to record the various shades of red that Sebastian's face had gone through! He was certainly very mad, but, just as certainly beaten. Reluctantly Sebastian signed the papers, before telephoning the bank and arranging the transfer of the money with immediate effect. I know I could have got a lot more, but I'd already had half a million in my bank account, from the money Sebastian had given me for 'pocket money' whilst we were still together. I had been saving it up for ages.

The most important thing to me was to get Sebastian out of my life forever and quickly. Taking only a small amount of money off him was worth it, to me it was priceless!

What was that saying about revenge being best served cold.? I waited in Sebastian's office until I received confirmation from my bank, that the money had been transferred, before getting up, collecting the divorce papers, picking up my suitcases, and, with head held high, walking out of the house, without so much as a backward glance. Once outside, I called a taxi to take me back to the hotel, and my Jensen.

I entered my hotel room, to see that Jensen was fast asleep in bed. The bed sheets were only covering the lower half of his body, and I could see his bare, muscular chest, popping out of the covers. He was wearing the angel necklace that I had bought him. He looked so peaceful. 'Chloe, you would have liked Jensen.' I thought to myself, as I looked out of the hotel window and up to the sky, and said 'Goodbye my precious angel.' I knew that she would be looking down on us from heaven, and at that moment, a rainbow lit the sky. I was sure it was a sign from Chloe, it had to be. She was always drawing rainbows, she always said that drawing rainbows made her happy! I climbed into bed beside Jensen and I held him close to me. I wanted to make him safe, just as he had me, so many times recently.

I soon fell asleep and found myself dreaming of Chloe. I dreamt that she was sitting on my bed, telling me that she was ok, that she was happy, and that she didn't need to draw rainbows anymore, as she was surrounded by real ones to play with. Even though I was asleep, I felt my heart lighten. A few hours later, Jensen and I woke up. Jensen asked me how long I'd been laid next to him as he hadn't heard me come in. I told him that I'd been laid next to him for a few hours. 'What have you been up to?' Jensen asked. 'Well, I met Uncle Timothy, who's a lawyer, who drew up my divorce papers to Sebastian, so I could give them to Sebastian when I went to see him. Which I might add, that he reluctantly signed. I made him transfer the divorce settlement money into my account whilst I sat in his office, you should have seen Sebastian's face, it was a picture!' I explained with a big smile on my face. 'After Chloe's funeral, I won't have to see him again. He'll be out of my life for good.' I continued. Jensen couldn't believe his ears, 'You've accomplished all that in such a short space of time? I'm so proud of you!' He announced. In all honesty, I was quite proud of myself too.

I went on to tell Jensen, how I'd looked out of the hotel window, and a rainbow suddenly appeared, and that Chloe loved rainbows. I told him about my dream. 'How do you know it was a dream? It could have really happened.' Jensen suggested. I liked that idea, that Chloe could have visited me to tell me that she was happy up in heaven. Jensen climbed from the bed and made us both a cup of tea from the hospitality tray in our room, before clambering back into bed, with a huge smile on his face. 'What are you smiling at?' I asked. 'Now Sebastian has agreed to a quickie divorce, and signed the papers, we'll be able to get married quite soon, if you still want to be with me!' Jensen announced. 'We'll have to wait a few weeks for the Decree Absolute to come through, but I certainly do want to marry you!' I told him, and we agreed to start making plans.

That evening we visited my parents at their house. I had persuaded Jensen to come along and meet them. He was very apprehensive, which is understandable, seeing as they'd never heard about him before. My mum was a bit taken aback at first, as I told her how we had met, and that I'd fallen in love with him and that we were going to be married. I think it was all a bit too much for her to take in, and she had to retire to her bedroom as she had a migraine. Although I was a bit annoyed at mums 'early retirement' I couldn't be too hard on her, after everything that had happened over the last few weeks, and decided that it was probably a good time for us to leave. My dad was surprisingly supportive. He usually kept quiet and did as he was told by my mother! He shook Jensen's hand warmly, on hearing the news of our impending wedding. He remarked how happy he was for the pair of us. I informed dad of the arrangements we'd made for Chloe, and that I was going to organise the flowers, in the morning. Chloe's death had aged my dad. He looked drained and heartbroken. I gave him a hug and we left.

On the way back to the hotel we called into an Italian restaurant that I Knew, as we hadn't eaten since breakfast, and I was getting a little hungry. We ordered pasta, and we chatted as we waited for it to arrive. I told Jensen all about Chloe, and the time that we spent together. And of the escapades we used to get up to. I wanted to talk to him in more depth about my life with Chloe, I felt Jensen had earned that right, having spent day after day with me at Chloe's bedside. Although I'd just said goodbye to Chloe at the hospital earlier that day, deep down I think I had always known what the eventual outcome was going to be. I just had a hard time facing up to the fact. Don't get me wrong, I never gave up on her like Sebastian had, nor had I given up hope of a miracle happening, and that she would wake up, and although I was extremely upset at losing her. I truly believe that my dream was heaven sent, and Chloe was letting me know that she was fine, and the angels were looking after her. Somehow, that made my pain more bearable. I think that I was still running on auto pilot to some degree, and although I appeared to be holding up well, I knew it was only a matter of time before I would crumble. I needed to be strong, so I could organise the arrangements and to be strong for my mum and dad, as they felt so guilty about Chloe's accident, seeing as she was in their care at the time. You could tell by the pain on their faces, that they blamed themselves and that this would torment them for years to come.

After eating our meal, we decided to go for a walk and take in the night air. People hurried and scurried past us, going about their business. Everybody seemed to be in one almighty rush. I hadn't missed this frantic pace of life one bit. In America, things seemed to be slower, and even more laid back in New England. I wondered what it was, I'd liked about being here in the first place. Back at the hotel, we decided to have an early night, as we'd a lot of people to see and arrangements to make the next day. Jensen offered to run me a bath, I think he had cottoned on to the fact that, I took baths not only to keep clean, but to de stress and re charge my batteries. Although our relationship was quite new, we were learning a lot about each other very quickly. We seemed to be evolving at the same rate and growing closer with every passing minute. He understood me more than anyone ever had before in my life. Probably because he'd taken the time to get to know me, time to see what made me tick. He could sense when I was feeling sad and vulnerable, and would often hold me close to comfort me and make me feel safe. He had an uncanny knack of knowing when I needed to be alone, to work things out for myself, and at times like that, he would let me know that he was there, waiting for me, should I need him. But still allowing me the space that I needed. I could count on one hand, the amount of friends that I had, who were married and could say that they've achieved what I'd had, with Jensen. And most of my friends had been married ten years or more. That was how I knew that Jensen and I would be together forever.

After a long soak in the bath, I emerged feeling a bit better. Jensen and I climbed in to bed. 'Can we make love?' I asked him. Jensen took my hand and looked at me, 'I don't want to rush you, I want you to wait until you're ready.' He replied in a hushed voice. I told him that I was ready. I had been sharing a bed with him for eight days and we hadn't done anything, because of everything that had been going on. I'd just needed him there to be supportive, as he had been, but now I needed him to make love to me, as tenderly as he usually did.

I needed the closeness of our lovemaking, I wanted to feel his hands on my skin, and touch his soft lips against my body. I needed a release that only he could deliver. We stood at the end of the bed, and his hands undid my bathrobe. It slipped to the floor. Jensen kissed me on the lips and on my face, then he slowly worked his way down, over my body, kissing every inch of me. Then he began to probe my moist slit with his tongue, then his fingers, bringing me to orgasm on both occasions. He walked behind me as I stood there all hot and bothered on the floor. He kissed my neck and shoulders, then moved down my spine to my lower back. His lips brushed over the skin on my bum. He kissed my thighs, then gently pushed my legs apart before exploring me with his mouth once more. I lost control and came again, cum dribbling down my thighs, he turned me towards him and laid me on the bed. Jensen lay beside me, his cock semi erect. I climbed on top of him and returned the compliment, kissing every inch of his body. I licked the length of his penis, and took him in my mouth, teasing him with my tongue and sucking on his penis until he came in my mouth. I pulled myself up, and moved towards his face, where I straddled him and pulled his head onto my wet mound, encouraging him to taste me once again. I came over and over again as his tongue darted in and out of me, probing the depths of my love hole, flicking my clitoris. My body ached and I was totally drained of cum. I pushed his face away and sat astride his big throbbing penis, which had made a quick comeback, and was standing to attention again following my previous oral explora-tion. I started to ride rhythmically on his long, very stiff penis, And it wasn't long before his pulsating tool exploded his seed into me. Jensen groaned in ecstasy on his release, and pulled me close to him, kissing me hard on the lips. We kissed until he was ready for another lovemaking session. He turned me over and took me from behind, his lovemaking got more demanding. Jensen pumped me harder and harder until we orgasmed together, and both fell exhausted on the bed.

Once we recovered from our epic lovemaking session, Jensen and I began talking about our future plans. I decided to fly back to New England with Jensen, as soon as it was possible, after the funeral. I planned to take Chloe's ashes back to America with me. I felt that was what she would have wanted, to be near her mummy. Seeing as Jensen and I were starting a new life together there. Jensen said that we could make part of his garden into a memorial area for Chloe, and we could plant some flowers and maybe a tree there, where we could scatter her ashes. Jensen told me that he would make a bench and place it nearby, so that I could go and sit and talk to Chloe, or just to go and remember the good times that we'd shared. I really liked that idea. I knew that the next few days would be really tough, but with Jensen by my side, I also knew that I'd get through it. Jensen and I snuggled up together and drifted off into a deep and contented sleep.

CHAPTER 7

The following morning I woke early as I had a lot of running around to do. Sebastian had already organised the funeral directors for me, and I was going to organise the flowers, the Eulogy, and arrange for Chloe's favourite song to be played at the service. Chloe had loved the song 'Walking on Sunshine' and used to dance around whatever room she was in at the time, skipping and jumping about to the music, whenever it was played on the radio. In fact, my dad had the song on a compilation CD at his house, and whenever Chloe went to visit, she would ask her grandad to play the 'sunshine song' as she called it. She would ask for it to be played over and over again. I think my dad got sick of playing it in the end, so on one of her visits he gave her the CD. Chloe was over the moon!

I bought Chloe a CD player for her to have in her bedroom, so she could listen to it whenever she wanted. I showed her how to press the repeat button on her CD player, so that she could play the song over and over again, to her heart's content. Although Chloe had only been very young, she had been very advanced with regards to technology, indeed, she'd been able to work her granddad's computer without any problems. Chloe only needed to be shown how to do something once and she would remember what to do straight away. Her brain had been like a giant sponge when it came to absorbing information on new technology.

I sat beside my hotel window, trying to write my Eulogy for Chloe. I was having difficulty putting into words what I wanted to say. I knew what I wanted to say, but when I wrote down the words, they didn't sound right. So I sat looking out of the window, waiting for some kind of inspiration. In the end I decided to write a poem to read out instead. The poem needed to reflect Chloe's character, it had to be a poem that would 'say' Chloe. What she was like, her likes, and her loves. My mind was blank. I sat back in my chair and closed my eyes, concentrating hard on the words to write. As if by magic, words started to appear in my mind:-

You were taken one day, upon a breeze,

Taken back to heaven, far above the trees,

To a place where angels sing, and rainbows are made,

With a blink of an eye, you had taken flight,

Back to the homestead, in heaven above,

Where you could share your inspiration and love.

In times of sadness, I see no light,

I have lost my little girl, who so bravely put up a fight,

I look for meaning, in this ever cruel world,

And look to God for answers, but do not hear.

Then, all of a sudden, the skies will clear,

And up pops a rainbow, to bring good cheer,

I know when I see one, that you are close,

Forever in my heart, you meant the most.

'That was it! That was what I would read at Chloe's funeral.' I thought. I woke Jensen and read my poem to him. He thought it was beautiful and we both agreed that Chloe would like the poem. We went to the florists. It was the florist who used to supply the flowers for the dinner parties that I used to organise for Sebastian and his business associates. I only chose that particular florist because I knew they would make a good job of the flowers, and that was important to me. Once we'd chosen the flowers, we dropped off our song choices for the funeral service, at the vicarage. Everything I needed to organise, had been organised, apart from letting people know the date and time of the service, but my dad said that he would do that. I couldn't face all the sympathy's that people offer. I wanted to make sure we celebrated Chloe's life at the service, after all she'd been a little girl who had em- braced life. We returned to the hotel room to relax a while, as I was quite drained. It was mid-afternoon when the telephone rang. It was my mum, phoning to let me know that Charlotte had flown in for the funeral, and that she'd left a message asking if we could meet up before the funeral service. Charlotte had told my mum that she wanted to clear the air, so there'd be no bad feeling at the funeral service. I didn't have the time, nor the inclination to hear her pathetic confessions, or give her my forgiveness, so that she could feel better. As far as I was concerned, she would deal with her guilty conscience on her own!

Jensen and I went into the city to do a spot of retail therapy. I wanted to buy him a suit for the funeral, as he hadn't thought that he was going to need one when he left America. He hadn't expected to be going to a funeral! I wanted to buy Jensen a suit, as he hadn't let me spend anything when I stayed at his house, and he must have spent a small fortune on taking me to the restaurant, the honeymoon suite, and my engagement ring! I knew he wasn't rich. He was a hardworking, ordinary guy who didn't have a lot, but what he did have, he was willing to share with me! We headed off to Harrods and picked out a grey suit which had a fine pinstripe running through it. Jensen really did look gorgeous in a suit. Mind you, Jensen could look good in anything. He was one of those people who didn't need to spend time making himself look good. He could wear a bin liner, and still look sexy! Whereas I, on the other hand, went out and bought the latest potions and lotions in the hope that they somehow, miraculously worked, and did exactly what they said they did on the bottle.

Makes you sick, doesn't it? I wish I was like those women who said that they embraced growing old gracefully, not worrying about colouring their hair when they saw a grey one, and being content with who they were, and what they saw staring back at them when they looked in the mirror. I wouldn't consider myself as vain, I just believe that you should care about how you look. If you ask any man who they would sooner go on a date with, a forty-one year old woman, with immaculate hair and nice clothes, or a forty-one year old woman with grey hair and sweat pants, which one do you think they'd choose? I rest my case! We'd arranged to meet my parents for a meal. I was dreading it actually, especially after the way my mother feigned one of her famous migraines when I'd introduced her to Jensen for the first time. I hoped she wasn't going to make Jensen feel uneasy when we met her later tonight. My mother was famous amongst her friends for speaking her mind. Sometimes she would say things that went too far, especially if she had a strong opinion about something. She certainly didn't mince her words, and I often wondered how she actually managed to keep her friends.

I remember the time that the daughter of one of her friends had fallen pregnant at seventeen. Everyone had tried to cover up the fact that she had decided not to keep the baby, and have a termination. But oh no! Not my mother. Whilst at a friend's barbeque, the girl in question turned up and everybody was trying to avoid the subject of her termination, everyone that was, except my mother. She loudly asked who had invited the slut, just loud enough for everyone to hear, and the girl ran off, in tears!

On the way back to the hotel to get changed, I decided that, should my mother make Jensen feel uncomfortable or uneasy, I was going to put her in her place, once and for all! After all, Jensen had been so supportive towards me. He even stayed by Chloe's bedside in the hospital, just in case she woke up from her coma, even though he hadn't met her before. All he knew about Chloe was what I'd told him about her. Jensen had stepped up to the plate more than Sebastian had, and Chloe was Sebastian's own daughter! Jensen hadn't abandoned her like, like Sebastian had. I wasn't in a great mood when we arrived at the hotel. I think it was because I'd psyched myself up, ready to explode at my mother if she dared speak out of turn, where Jensen was concerned. To be honest, I'd thought about cancelling the evening, but Jensen being his usual, understanding self, convinced me that we should go. 'It might be good to clear the air before the funeral.' He said, and he was right, as usual.

I couldn't be bothered to get dressed up, so I put on a pair of black trousers and a white, fitted blouse. 'It'll do.' I thought, as I looked in the mirror on the way out of the hotel room. The restaurant was busy when we arrived, and I was having difficulty finding my parents. 'Perhaps we should have arranged to meet somewhere else, they mustn't have arrived!' I thought to myself. Suddenly I spotted two familiar faces through the crowd. Not my parents, but Sebastian and Charlotte! They looked cosy, very cosy indeed! Jensen must have sensed my trepidation, as he carefully slipped his arm around my waist and pulled me to him. 'What's wrong?' He whispered. Of course, Jensen didn't know what Sebastian or Charlotte looked like, so he didn't realise that they were there. As I explained to Jensen, my parents walked into the restaurant, and called out to me. Upon hearing my mother's bellowing voice calling me across the room, Sebastian looked around in absolute horror! Sebastian glanced around the room, and as his gaze met mine he seemed to sink into his seat, hoping that I hadn't spotted him, or Charlotte. Unfortunately, I had!

We ordered our drinks at the bar, and as my mother went off to pass pleasantries with Sebastian, I turned to my dad. 'Please don't tell me mother has invited those two.' I asked. Dad nodded, he was embarrassed. He explained that he'd tried to tell her it was a bad idea, but she'd refused to listen. I reached for my coat, 'I'm not going to stay here playing happy families just for my mother's sake.' I told him. My dad grabbed my arm, and begged me to stay, for his sake. If I'd left, my dad would have been in the doghouse as usual. Jensen turned to me and squeezed my hand. 'Come on,' he said. 'we can get through this. Let's just stay for your dad's sake.' Reluctantly I agreed, and as I put down my coat, my dad thanked Jensen for getting me to stay. The waiter arrived and called us all to our table. 'This is going to be fun!' I thought. I took a deep breath, and walked towards our table. My mother grabbed Sebastian's arm, and loudly told him that he could sit next to her. I glanced towards my dad. He beckoned Jensen over, 'Come and sit next to me son.' He told Jensen. My dad had played a blinder, my mother, Sebastian, and that scheming bitch, Charlotte all sat with their mouths wide open, in total surprise at my dad calling Jensen, 'son'. Not once in all the time Sebastian and I had been together, had my dad ever called Sebastian 'son'. It was sure to have hit home and made a point. I was so pleased. Sebastian ended up sitting next to my mother, with Charlotte beside him, whilst my dad, Jensen, and I sat opposite them. 'Well, battle lines have certainly been drawn!' I thought, as my mother gave my dad a stare of disapproval. My dad went round the table, doing the introductions, so that Jensen would know who everyone was. Sebastian, in his 'up his own arse', self-assured way, asked Jensen who he was, and where he came from. I saw my mother opening her mouth to reply, as she liked to do, but before she could utter a word, I replied that Jensen was, in fact, my new partner and that he came from America. Sebastian and Charlotte both choked on their wine as they took a sip. 'You didn't mention him when you came over to mine.' Announced Charlotte, who seemed a little put out by the fact!

'Why would I? Why didn't you tell me that you had been sleeping with Sebastian for the last so many years, until I came to see you!' I retorted. My dad looked at me and grinned broadly, like The Cheshire cat, from Alice in Wonderland, as if to say, well done, you put her in her place! Sebastian began to inter-rogate Jensen about how, and when we'd met. He hated not knowing everybody's business, and I think that was probably one of the reasons why he and my mother got on so well with each other. I was really proud of the way Jensen refused to rise to Sebastian's bait. Jensen simply told Sebastian that it wasn't any of his business, and that he was glad we'd met as he was madly in love with me. The remainder of the evening went off without any major drama. My mother was unusually quiet for a change, I think she was shocked at my dad's defence of Jensen. I had never known my dad to do that before. He was always so placid, doing everything my mother asked, no, told him to do, and for my dad to defend Jensen meant something.

My mother realised this, she knew that my dad was a man of few words, and that when he spoke up, his word was final! At the end of the meal my dad shook Jensen's hand and welcomed him into the family, telling Jensen that he was proud to call him his son. I glanced across at Sebastian with a wry smile on my face. I could see how my dad's comments had infuriated him. That really did please me! We said our 'goodnight's' and walked out of the restaurant, I felt eight feet tall. Jensen asked if I was okay. I smiled and nodded, and took Jensen's arm. I was so proud of the way Jensen had handled Sebastian's questioning, and how he remained dignified, yet firm with Sebastian, as if to let him know that, no matter how Sebastian tried to intimidate him, it wouldn't work. Sebastian's obvious disapproval of our relationship hadn't unnerved Jensen at all. Jensen had stood his ground and declared his love for me, and that made me feel so good! The night was mild, so we decided to take a stroll around the park, before heading back to the hotel. The skies were clear of clouds and the stars twinkled like sparkling diamonds, quite beautiful to look at. It was quite a serene and peaceful moment. The park was empty, but for a couple of people walking their dogs, and a couple sat huddled together on a park bench, holding hands and looking lovingly into one another's eyes. Jensen placed his arm around my shoulders and pulled me close, as we walked through the park. Jensen made me feel wanted, needed, and most of all, loved. I hadn't really felt this way before, and I liked the way he made me feel. It was perfect! I was frightened that my bubble of happiness might burst and I would wake up in the realisation that, it had all been a dream. I saw Jensen looking at me. I knew that he could tell that I was feeling nervous and apprehensive. He stopped in front of me. 'What's wrong?' He enquired. I told him nothing was wrong, trying to get him off the scent. I didn't want him to know how fragile I felt, but Jensen being Jensen, wasn't having any of it. 'Look, I know you too well, what's the matter? People don't go around with tears welling in their eyes for no reason at all!' He declared. I hadn't noticed that I had tears in my eyes. 'Look!' I said, 'It's just that good things don't usually happen to me and when they do, I start to wonder if it's all been a dream. I've really fallen head over heels in love with you, and I've been quite shocked at how it's happened so fast. I'm just afraid that you'll get fed up with me. Look at the things you are having to deal with.' 'Like what?' Jensen enquired. 'Like having my mother invite

Sebastian to dinner, and him questioning you. I worry that it will all become too much for you, and you'll leave me!' Jensen shook his head and told me that he would never feel that way about me. That I had a heart of gold, and how I was really special to him. He said that he would follow me to the ends of the earth and beyond. He said that he couldn't imagine his life without my being in it, and that's the way it would stay! He pulled me to him and gently and tenderly kissed me. His soft lips made my mouth tingle, and, like magic, every part of my body followed suit. My face and neck began to get hot, and I could feel myself burning up. I felt as though I was melting. My legs began to quiver. I needed to sit down before I fell down. The way Jensen kissed me, took my breath away. My head spun and I felt dizzy with passion. We finished kissing. Jensen wiped away my tears and kissed me on the nose. We continued to walk through the park. I didn't want to go back to the hotel, so we flagged down a taxi and asked the driver to take us to Brighton. When we arrived in Brighton, we made our way to the seafront. The beach was empty, but we still carried on walking towards the sandy shore. We took off our shoes and strolled hand in hand along the sand. We could see that the tide was out as we stood facing out to sea. The cool coastal breeze gently tickled our faces. 'This is heavenly.' I thought. I enjoyed visiting Brighton of an evening, to take a walk along the deserted beach. During the day, the beach heaved with half naked bodies all vying for the best spot to get a suntan. Looking onto the beach from the promenade during the day, the bathers looked like sardines, all huddled together. It was certainly more peaceful and relaxing at this time of night! We walked for what seemed like miles, until our feet could carry us no further. We sat down on the sand and gazed up at the moon glowing in the night sky and listening to the distant ebb of the waves.

We decided to stay on the beach until we saw the sun rise, so we lay down on the beach and held each other close. I leant over Jensen's body and started to kiss him. I kissed his mouth, then his face and ears. I'd never made love on a beach before, and it was an experience that I wanted to share with Jensen! I unbuttoned his shirt and kissed his chest, nuzzling his nipples with my mouth, which made him start to groan. His moans spurred me on to examine the rest of his body with my mouth. He carried on groaning in pleasure, which in turn made me want to make him moan some more. I undid his trousers to reveal his long, hard cock! I licked up and down the length of his shaft, and he started to juice. I took him in my mouth and started to tease his tip with my tongue, gently flicking at it. As I worked on the end of his penis, Jensen let out an almighty moan of pleasure and exploded into my mouth. He pushed my body into the sand as he leant over me, kissing my lips hard. I could hear his heavy breathing, as he started to unbutton my blouse. His hands traced every inch of my breasts, before he took my erect nipples into his mouth, one at a time. Flicking and sucking them hard with his tongue, making me tingle all over, with his touch. He removed my trousers and started to rub my groin over my thong, gasping, as he inserted his fingers into my briefs. I knew he could tell, how turned on I was. I was wet with anticipation of his touch. He slipped two fingers into my aching pussy, and firmly brought me off in his hand. Jensen slid his fingers out of my love hole and he started to tease my clitoris. I could feel the passion running through my body once more, as he brought me to orgasm once more. He climbed on top of me and slowly filled my waiting pussy with his throbbing manhood. Pushing himself so deeply inside me, that I cried out his name. I held onto Jensen's back as he raised my legs over his shoulders. He began to make love to me with more urgency. His rhythm became more intense as we came together. I felt as though my body was going to explode! I didn't think that I'd anymore love juice left in me. He turned me over and made love to me from behind. His hands gripped my waist as he thrust himself in and out of me, his cock was still as hard as ever. My pussy ached, as he rammed me, relentlessly.

I could feel every contour, every ridge of his penis, as he moved back and forth between my legs. Jensen slowed his pace and began to ride me, and a few moments later, we climaxed together. We collapsed on the sand, both gulping at the sea air, searching for breath. My legs were quivering and every nerve ending in my body twitched, as we lay naked on the sand. holding each other and looking up into the clear, starlit skies. We picked up our clothes and moved them further up the beach, towards the wall of the promenade as the tide was just starting to come in. We then ran into the sea and washed our lovemaking session away. The sea was freezing cold, but very refreshing after such an exhausting lovemaking session. Once clean, we made our way up onto the beach.

We picked our clothes up and quickly got dressed, then walked up onto the promenade and sat looking out to sea. The sun was just starting to come up. I leant my head on Jensen's shoulder and we watched the sun come up over the sea, it was bliss. Behind us, we could hear someone opening some shop shutters. I turned and saw that a small cafe was just opening up. We walked across to the cafe and peered inside and asked the cafe owner if she was open yet. The lady invited us inside, and we ordered two full English breakfasts and two mugs of tea. The lady saw that we were dripping with water. 'Late night?' She enquired, 'Oh yes, a very late night!' I said. Lovemaking with Jensen, always gave me a good appetite. We hurriedly tucked into our breakfasts, enjoying every mouthful. We drank our tea's and ordered two more, then sat and chatted a little while longer. Today was Chloe's funeral. We asked the cafe owner if she could call us a taxi, to take us back to the hotel so we could get ready.

A part of me was dreading today. Chloe's funeral, made things so final. I looked at Jensen and knew that he would give me the strength that I needed, to get through the day. About ten minutes later, our taxi pulled up outside. We paid for our breakfasts and set off back to the hotel. On our return to the hotel room, Jensen and I had a shower. There was still a few hours to go before Chloe's funeral. We sat by the window, it had turned out to be a beautiful sunny day. I was glad, I wouldn't have wanted to be saying my final goodbyes to Chloe on a miserable day. Chloe was never miserable, she always had been such a happy child, always laughing, with such a sunny disposition. Today's weather summed up Chloe. I just wanted to sit by the window for a while and gather my thoughts. I took a deep breath, as I felt the tears begin to well in my eyes. I had a heavy heart, I felt as though my heart had been ripped out of my body. A part of me was missing and would always be. I never imagined that I'd be holding a funeral for my daughter. I always expected to go first, as all parents do, not the other way round! I promised myself that, today I wouldn't be sad, although I obviously was. Chloe wouldn't want us to be sad, she'd want us to celebrate her short, but happy life. To talk about her little escapades, her cute take on life, and the things she loved. Today, I wasn't going to let her down. Today, I would hold back my tears and talk about all the happy times we'd had together. My thoughts were interrupted by the sound of the telephone ringing. I picked up the receiver, it was my dad, checking if everything was alright as he had been trying to ring me at the hotel since last night, when we had left the restaurant. My dad apologised for my mother's behaviour and had said that he told my mother that she had no right to interfere, my dad assured me that it wouldn't happen again. I thanked him and wondered how long this minor miracle would last, my mother wouldn't be able to help herself, she always had to interfere in other people's business. My dad offered to pick us up from the hotel and take us to the funeral, but I declined, saying that Jensen and I would make our own way there. My dad went onto explain that, Sebastian had invited him and mum to travel in one of the funeral cars with him and Charlotte. My dad declined, saying that it wouldn't be appropriate as I wasn't travelling in the cortege. Sebastian had also said that I would also be welcomed to join them. What a bloody cheek! Did Sebastian think that I would accompany him and Charlotte in the main funeral car? I had no intention of sharing a car with Sebastian, and even less intention of travelling alongside Charlotte. As far as I was concerned, Charlotte had no business attending the funeral at all. She wasn't Chloe's mother, I was. I decided that I was going to put Charlotte in her place if she attempted to sit in one of the pews that was just reserved for family. She wasn't family, just a husband stealing floosie! I wasn't going to let 'Charlotte the harlot' inflict anymore sadness on my family. It was going to be a difficult enough day as it was, without her causing any further upset.

Jensen could tell that I was fuming, when I got off the telephone. I told him what had been said, and he told me not to get worked up about it, as he would have a quiet word with Charlotte and suggest that she should sit next to him in one of the pews behind the family members. I didn't relish the thought of Charlotte sitting next to Jensen. She might attempt to ruin my relationship with him, after all, she had gone after my husband! I wouldn't put anything past her. I knew that I was being silly, Jensen loved me and wouldn't do anything as low as that. It wasn't him that I didn't trust, it was Charlotte. I returned to my seat by the window. I picked up the poem that I'd written, to read in church, and read the words again to ensure that it said all I wanted to say, it did. 'Chloe would be proud.' I thought. As I sat sipping the coffee that Jensen had made me, the sky lit up with colour. I rose from my chair to see what was illuminating the sky. To my surprise and delight, it was the biggest, brightest rainbow that I've ever seen. It stretched over the whole sky, and I couldn't make out where the rainbow started or where it finished. I was quite taken aback at the beauty of it.

I called out to Jensen, who was in the bathroom, and he came running into the room. I pointed out of the window at the rainbow, and in unison, we both declared that it was Chloe making a rainbow to cheer us up, and to let us know that she was up above, watching over us! Seeing the rainbow, seemed to calm my nerves somehow, I felt it was a sign that things would be okay. I called a local limousine firm and asked if they had a car available as I needed one in a couple of hours time, to attend a funeral. And as luck would have it, they did so I gave them all the details and arranged for them to pick up Jensen and I. As I sorted my funeral attire out, Jensen said that he needed to pop out for a while, as there was something that he needed to do. He promised to be back in time for the limousine picking us up. He kissed me and headed out of the door.

I got dressed and put on my make up, then rang the flower shop to see if the flowers that I'd ordered had been delivered to the church. The florist told me not to worry as everything had been delivered already. As I put the phone down, a knock came on the door. I opened it and saw Sebastian standing there. I asked him what he wanted and how he knew where to find me. Apparently my mother had told him at the restaurant last night, where I was staying. Sebastian wanted to know where Jensen was, was it serious with him and would I be prepared to give Sebastian another chance. I couldn't believe what I was hearing. 'Give it another go! Not bloody likely!' I told him. 'I thought Charlotte was the love of your life.' I added sarcastically. He shook his head, knowing Sebastian as well as I did, I doubted that he wanted me back, he just didn't like losing. He'd always been the one, who said what went on, in our marriage, and like a fool, I'd always gone along with it. But not this time, this time I was in control of my own destiny, and my destiny was with Jensen. I told Sebastian, as politely as I could, without using any expletives, to go. He did, with his pride in tatters!

Although it might seem childish, I was glad his pride was hurt, I proved to myself what I'd known for such a long time, that I was over him. I could get on with re building my life with someone who mattered, and Jensen mattered a lot. Jensen returned a few minutes later and I told him about Sebastian's visit, and what he'd come for. Jensen handed me a small box, I opened it. Inside was a brooch of a rainbow and it was en-crusted with semi precious stones. It was beautiful. Jensen explained that he saw it when we'd been out shopping, a few days before and that he just had to go back and buy it for me. Jensen took the brooch out of the box and pinned it onto my jacket collar. I threw my arms around him and gave him a kiss. 'Thank you' I whispered, just as the phone rang. It was the hotel receptionist letting us know that the limousine had arrived to collect us.

CHAPTER 8

We arrived at the church. It was full of people who I'd not seen for years. Even some of my ex-work colleagues from the bank, had taken the time to pay their respects. Some of them I worked with before I married Sebastian. I made my way to the front of the church and saw Charlotte sitting next to Sebastian, just as I'd predicted she would. We made eye contact, and I glared at her. I wasn't impressed, not impressed at all. She leaned over and whispered to Sebastian that she thought she ought to move, and before Sebastian could protest, Jensen had ushered her out of the pew and down the aisle towards the back of the church, where they both sat down. I felt that Jensen had earned the right to sit next to me up front, as he'd spent so much time at the hospital with me, as I waited for Chloe to wake from her coma. Jensen told me that it was only right that Sebastian and I sat together, as we were Chloe's parents. He was probably right!

I took my seat and, as I looked up, I saw Chloe's coffin. It was so small, and the top was adorned with small pink flowers. Although Chloe's coffin was white, the sun shone through the stained glass windows of the church, giving it the appearance of being rainbow coloured. I thought that was very apt. Chloe's song started to play. I glanced over at my dad and could see that he was visibly upset. He and Chloe used to listen to that song all the time, I gave him a smile, to reassure him. My lips started to quiver with emotion, and I had a lump in my throat. I was finding it difficult to breathe and felt that I couldn't swallow, all of my throat ached and the room started to spin, the next thing I knew, I was on the floor coming round, with Jensen and my dad at my side. I'd fainted, under the stress and upset of the situation. I was helped to my feet and back onto the pew, where I'd been sitting. My dad suggested that Jensen sat next to me, to steady me. Jensen took my hand and sat beside me.

I apologised to the vicar, who told me not to worry. He asked me if it was ok to proceed, and with tears in my eyes I nodded my head yes. Chloe's favourite song started to play once more, and the vicar started to tell everyone about Chloe. He told everyone how he'd baptised her, here in this very church, and that it was so sad that Chloe had lost her life at such an early age. He said that it was a sad time for all of us. He went on to tell everyone how he'd got to know Chloe very well as she was a regular at the weekly service. Explaining how she would light up the church, when she skipped in on a Sunday. The vicar said that wherever she went, she had a strong presence. He was certainly right about that! The time came for me to address the congregation, I made my way to the pulpit and looked out at all the people in church, who had turned up to pay their respects to Chloe. I was overwhelmed. I started to read out the poem that I'd written for Chloe, but as I read the words, my voice began to falter. I had to clear my throat and start again. I kept telling myself to be strong. I was finding it hard, but managed to read my poem. As I looked up at the congregation, there wasn't a dry eye in the church. Even my mother had tears in her eyes, and as far as I could remember, she'd never shown any emotion in life. I climbed down from the pulpit, feeling warm inside that Chloe had touched so many people's hearts. It was my dad's turn next, and he went on to tell everyone about all the mischief, he and Chloe used to get up to. Some of the things he described were so funny, that people chuckled out loud. I was pleased that Chloe's antics had made people laugh, and I knew Chloe would have felt the same.

Finally, it came to the part of the service where the curtains closed around Chloe's coffin, my resolve crumbled and I sobbed uncontrollably. I didn't want to let my baby go, I wasn't ready. Jensen held on to me, supporting me, even though he had tears in his eyes and was upset too. I cried out for Chloe, and those around me tried to calm me down. I attempted to run towards Chloe's coffin, but the vicar held on to me, to prevent me from going any further. He told me that he was sorry for my loss, but Chloe was going back home to god. That wasn't what I wanted to hear. I wanted Chloe to come home with me. The vicar beckoned Jensen over, and asked him to take me back to my seat, but I couldn't bear it. I just wanted to get out of the church, as far away as possible! I rushed from the church with Jensen at my side, closely followed by my parents. All I could say was, 'I'm sorry', over and over again. All I really wanted was to be strong, but the whole experience of saying goodbye to my Chloe was too much for me to bear. I climbed into the limousine and we headed back to the hotel. I just couldn't face going back to Sebastian's house after the funeral. He'd organised some caterer's to come in and put on a spread, but I didn't want to go and stuff my face with food. I wanted to hide away and grieve for my precious daughter.

Once back at the hotel, Jensen organised some strong, sugary tea for me. Apparently it was supposed to be good for shock. It was probably an old wives tale, and found not to be true. Jensen ran me a bath and helped me to undress. I felt like a zombie. I couldn't think straight, I just wanted to go to sleep and not wake up! I soaked in the bath, until the water had turned cold. Jensen helped me out of the bath, dried me, and put me to bed. He'd been a real star. I don't know what I would have done without him. He made me another strong, sugary tea and as I sipped it, Jensen rang my dad. He let him know that we were back at the hotel, and that I was going to rest. Jensen promised my dad that he'd phone him in the morning, to let him know how I was. Jensen sat on the bed beside me, and stroked my forehead until I fell asleep. I must have slept for hours as it had started to get dark when I awoke. Jensen was sat in the chair beside the window, looking at me, watching over me. He had a worried expression on his face. I could see that he was concerned about me. I could tell by the way he acted towards me. I apologised to him for making such a spectacle of myself. 'There's no need to apologise,' he kindly told me. 'it's understandable that things have begun to get to you, I've been waiting for this to happen. You've been trying to hold your emotions in, and be strong for everyone else, but you have to grieve eventually, it's only natural.' He continued.

Jensen was so mature in his outlook. He seemed to understand how people thought and how they behaved. He was older and wiser than his age would suggest. I think that's why I bonded so easily with him, from the first moment we met. He knew how to treat a woman, and he wasn't afraid to show his emotions, and he wasn't afraid of commitment! Jensen suggested that we should get something to eat. 'You need to keep your strength up!' He said. He was right. I did feel drained, like I had no energy. We hadn't eaten anything since breakfast, and that had been at six thirty this morning, in Brighton! I didn't fancy going out for a meal. I didn't want to mix with lots of people, so we decided we'd go to the nearby deli, and get some sandwiches. I fancied taking a stroll in the evening air, instead of being cooped up in our hotel room. I got dressed and we went to the deli, where I ordered my favourite sandwich, mature cheddar, celery and grapes, on malted bread. Jensen ordered a ham salad, crusty baguette. We sat inside, at a small table in one of the corners of the deli, and ate our food. Once we'd eaten, and as the night was still young, we did a bit of window shopping, browsing the closed shops. We stopped at one of the travel agents, and looked at an advert inviting people to visit America. I knew that we'd have to make plans to return to America, but I needed to collect Chloe's ashes first, and visit my parents, before jetting off to start my new life with Jensen. I scanned the adverts in the travel agent's window and saw that there were some special offers being advertised, encouraging people to take a relaxing break. 'Oh, I could just do with one of those at the moment. In fact Jensen could probably do with a break just as much as I did,' I thought. 'I might surprise him and go and book us a break when the shops open tomorrow!'

We walked and walked, I could feel myself starting to relax a little. I liked walking, it helped me to clear away the mental clutter in my head and put things into perspective. I had decided that I needed to move forward, not dwell on the past anymore, it wasn't doing me any good. Jensen asked me if I'd like to visit my parents, as he thought that it might do us all some good. 'Your dad's been so worried about you. Paying him a visit might set his mind at ease.' He suggested. 'Yes, I suppose you're right, let's go and see them, I don't want them worrying about me.' I replied. Jensen hailed a passing taxi and we set off to see my parents. We reached their house just after 8 O'clock. I rang the doorbell and waited for the door to be answered. I could hear the padding of feet on the tiled, hallway floor then the door opened. It was my mum. She wasn't her usual, critical self, she appeared genuinely pleased to see us. She was mild mannered and polite, and I was taken by surprise at her new attitude. Mum ushered us inside and called out to my dad as she did so. Dad met us in the hallway and gave me a big hug, then shook Jensen's hand before leading us into the lounge, where my mother brought in a tray filled with coffee and cakes and put them on the coffee table in front of us. I was amazed at my mother's transformation, I secretly wondered if my father had traded her in for a 'Stepford wife'! I looked at her face, and in some way it had softened. Gone were the frown lines, which I had always been convinced were due to her face muscles constantly being set in 'disapproving look' mode, due to the amount of things with which she didn't agree. I know that sounds awful, but there were many things she didn't approve of!

My mum poured the drinks, and offered the first cup to Jensen. 'I'm glad that you two have popped round, I've something I have to discuss with you.' She announced. 'Oh here goes.' I thought, but I was surprisingly wrong. 'I'd just like to apologise to you Jensen, for being so bloody minded and rude the other day at the restaurant, and apologise to both of you for inviting Sebastian and Charlotte to the restaurant. I know it's no excuse, but I find it hard to accept change. I want life as I know it, a life that remains the same, Sebastian and Arabella together, and frequent visits from Chloe!' Mum had tears in her eyes and her voice trembled as she spoke, and I knew then that she was speaking from the heart. 'The way I've treated Jensen is unforgivable.' She told us. I had to agree with her there!

She went on to explain that it wasn't a reflection of her opinion of Jensen, but more of an 'I don't want things to change' attitude. My dad piped up, explaining that he and my mother had been talking, and that he'd pointed out a few home truths to her, that they'd already lost a granddaughter and didn't want to push me away and lose a daughter too, especially as I was the only family that they had left. 'We can tell that you and Jensen are obviously very much in love, and we'd like to be a part of your future. Sebastian has treated you terribly, carrying on with your best friend and he certainly won't be welcomed in this house again!' My dad explained, looking towards my mother, who agreed with him totally.

Jensen thanked them for their kind words. 'You're welcome to share in our new life together.' And turning to my mother, asked 'Does that mean I get to call you mom?' My mother blushed, but by the expression on her face, I knew that she was pleased, flattered in fact. It had been good to clear the air, I didn't want to leave England without making the peace. We sat and talked for a couple of hours, my mother even got the dreaded photo albums out, and she showed Jensen photo's they'd taken of me as I was growing up. Some of the pictures made me squirm when I saw them.

Did I really go around with the big hair and frilly blouses? We all laughed at the pictures, and it was a nice, welcome break from the upset of the last few days. Jensen was right, it had done us all good. My mother had accepted that I'd moved on from my marriage to Sebastian, and she was finally giving Jensen a chance to show her just how nice he really was! as mum and dad saw us to the taxi at the end of the night, they asked us when we were thinking of going back to America. 'We're going to the travel agents in the morning to see what flights are available, but we will let you know our plans.' I told them. Dad closed the taxi door behind us and said 'Goodbye.' As we drove off in the taxi I thanked Jensen for suggesting the visit to my parents. 'I feel so much better and it was good to clear the air.' I told him, as I snuggled into his shoulder, all the way back to the hotel, counting my blessings and happy in the knowledge that I would be spending the rest of my life with Jensen.

Back at the hotel we had a couple of drinks in the lounge. A pianist was entertaining the guests and I thought back to the first date Jensen and I had, at my hotel in New England, there had been a pianist there too! That was when Jensen and I danced closely for the first time, and the first time we'd made love. As quite an old sentimental at heart, I often reflected on past times that had made me happy. Little did I know then, on our first date, that we'd be where we are now, planning our lives together! We finished our drinks and went back to our room, I was quite tired. I think staying awake on the beach in Brighton had exhausted me. Not that I was complaining, after all we were making new memories to share together. We both climbed into bed and fell fast asleep, holding each other close.

It was morning, I woke early, leaving Jensen to catch up on his sleep. I quickly got dressed and headed off to the travel agency, leaving Jensen a note explaining that I had to nip out, but wouldn't be long. I wanted to book a holiday as a surprise for him. I wasn't sure where I wanted to take him, just somewhere relaxing, with lots of sunshine. The lady at the travel agents showed me lots of offers, but none of them seemed ideal. One of her colleagues then shouted over to us that she knew of a fantastic holiday to the Maldives, the only trouble was that the flight was departing tonight. She showed me the details. It looked perfect, exactly what I was looking for. We would have our own wooden villa on the beach, with a terrace that opened onto its own private stretch of beach, the terrace even had its own whirlpool outside.

I rang my dad to tell him about it. I wanted to run a few things by him first, before I booked it. I explained that I wanted to book a break for Jensen, but I wasn't sure how I was going to get our suitcases, and Chloe's ashes, back to America. The travel agent told me that she could put together a package that would let us fly out from England, but allow us to return to New England, instead of having to fly back to the United Kingdom. My dad promised to collect the suitcases that I'd previously packed, containing

Chloe and I's things, from Sebastian's house on his way to pick us up from our hotel. He told me that he would also collect Chloe's ashes for me, and to make sure that everything arrived safely in America, he and my mother would fly out to New England with them, after we'd had our holiday. It seemed like a great idea, so I booked the holiday there and then, and booked my parents flight for a week later, so they could come and see me in my new home.

I left the travel agents on a high. 'I wonder what Jensen would say to my impulsively booked holiday?' I thought. I rushed around the shops, hastily buying suntan lotions, insect repellent, new bikini's, and holiday clothes, not to mention a few items of lingerie. I purchased swimming trunks and holiday clothes for Jensen too, then made my way back to the hotel. I'd bought my travellers cheques and currency from the travel agents, and my dad had offered to pick us up and take us to the airport. Everything was done, except my telling Jensen that was!

When I returned to the hotel room, Jensen was still asleep. 'He must need it, for him to still be sleeping this long.' I thought. I was glad he was still asleep, as he wouldn't know that I'd been out and arranged a surprise holiday, which would make it an even bigger surprise! All I needed to do now was to hide all the new clothes that I'd just bought. I repacked both of our suitcases, placing the new clothes at the bottom of the cases and putting our 'old' clothes back on top. I was hoping Jensen wouldn't see them. I'd just finished packing the cases as Jensen started to stir from his sleep. I walked over to the bed and kissed him on the cheek. He opened his eyes and smiled at me. He had a gorgeous smile. Had I mentioned that before? I rang down to reception and ordered room service, and for a change, I ran Jensen a hot bath. It was his turn to be pampered by me, just my way of saying thank you for being so supportive to me. Jensen climbed out of bed, revealing his tanned, firm, muscular body, he was certainly pleasing on the eye, especially mine! He strolled into the bathroom and eased himself into the hot water. He sighed and said, 'Ah, bliss!' as I started to wash him all over. As I massaged his back, Jensen reached over and pulled me, fully clothed, into the bath. He kissed me. 'Good morning.' He said. I was soaked, and every time I tried to get out of the bath, Jensen pulled me back in. In the end I gave up and stayed in the bath, dressed, and soaking wet from head to toe! The bath water had spilled over the sides of the bath as we frolicked, and there was water all over the bathroom floor. It was a good job the bathroom floor was tiled.

Jensen slowly and gently undressed me, his lips never leaving mine, not even for a second. Then he cupped my breasts with his hands as his fingers teased my nipples. He traced a path to my groin with his fingers and began to explore me, as I began to massage him all over with the creamy lather of the soap, before taking his erect penis in my hand and massaging it too, with the creamy lather of the soap. As I massaged him, Jensen's penis seemed to grow in my hand. It was already erect, but my massaging seemed to make it grow longer and firmer! There was just enough room in the bath for me to straddle him, which I did, slowly going up and down on his penis with my teased, and aching pussy, our lips remaining together all the while. Our kissing became more frantic as his tongue darted in and out of my mouth as he explored every part of it. Jensen's hands were now around my hips, pulling me further down onto him, pushing himself deeper into me with every stroke, as his pace grew ever quicker. I took hold of his hands so that he couldn't dictate the pace of our lovemaking. I wanted to take control, I wanted to make love to him slowly. I wanted Jensen to feel every inch of me, I wanted him to feel his penis slipping slowly into my now swollen pussy, to feel my muscles as they contracted and relaxed their grip on his throbbing penis. I wanted to build him up to such a crescendo, that it would leave his body tingling all over. Just as he did mine, whenever he made love to me. It wasn't long before I got my wish, as I felt his manhood jerk and pulsate, as he filled me with his seed. With every pulse as he shot his seed into me, he gasped out with pleasure, and his hands clasped tightly around my buttocks, his nails digging into my skin. We gazed into each other's eyes and whispered 'I love you' to one another, before stepping out of the bath. I put on a bathrobe and left the bathroom. Just as I did so there was a knock on the door, followed by the voice of a man calling out 'Room service!' I answered the door, as Jensen dried himself off. I signed for the food and wheeled the trolley into the room, as the waiter bid me 'goodbye' and left.

I put the tray of croissants, pastries, and pancakes onto the table, together with the pot of coffee. I called out to Jensen, to let him know that breakfast was ready. As he walked into the room he laughed. 'I thought that I'd just had breakfast!' He quipped, giving my bum a loving pat as he walked past me, to the table. I looked at him across the table as he tucked into his breakfast. I always seemed to be sneaking a look at him these days, but with every look I took, the sexier he became to me. I felt like I had a bad case of lust, but I couldn't help it. He made me feel like a real woman, and that feeling was nice, and not something that I was used to. They do say that you can't get enough of a good thing, don't they? I certainly planned on getting a lot more of Jensen, if you know what I mean! After breakfast, I told Jensen that I'd organised a surprise for him. He looked a little puzzled, as he didn't know that I'd sneaked out to the travel agents earlier that morning. 'How did you manage to organise a surprise without leaving the room?' He asked. I told him that I had my ways and that he would have to wait until later to get his surprise, as I needed to do a few things first. We both got dressed and travelled into the city. Today, Jensen had dressed casually. He was wearing the same jeans and denim jacket, that he'd worn when I'd first met him on the plane. God, he looked gorgeous, good enough to eat, and ooh did I want to eat him! I had to go to the bank to make sure that everything was in order, that the money Sebastian had transferred into my bank account, was available immediately. I wouldn't have been surprised if Sebastian hadn't recalled the money transfer, because

I'd told him that I didn't want to try again, or give our marriage another go. Thankfully, everything was in order at the bank. I was glad that I was almost free of him. With him signing the quickie divorce papers that my uncle had drawn up and the fact that, he wasn't contesting any part of it, meant that within a few weeks I would be totally free of him. Thank god! I had plans for some of the money, a sort of wedding gift to Jensen, but I was going to keep it a secret. I needed to enrol the help of Jensen's friends, the ones that Jensen had introduced me to, the day we went on a picnic by the lake. We went to lunch, where Jensen asked what kind of wedding I would like. 'I just want something simple, not large scale, as my wedding to Sebastian had been. I just want a few personal friends and close family.' Jensen suggested we should pop and see his dad who lived in Hove, as he wanted to formerly introduce me to him. He was going to introduce me as his fiancée! I liked the sound of that. I told Jensen that we ought to go and see him today, as we would be leaving for America soon, and it would be nice to meet him. Jensen phoned his dad who confirmed he would be in, so we took a taxi to Hove, to Jensen's dads.

We arrived at Jensen's dad's house. It was huge, a large Georgian property that oozed sophistication. We rang the doorbell and Jensen's dad opened the door. He was an older version of Jensen, quite good looking for his age, and had the same warm temperament as Jensen. He ushered both of us into the large drawing room, and asked his housekeeper to make us all some tea.

Jensen introduced me to his dad and, as promised, told him that I was his fiancée. His dad looked me up and down and told Jensen that he'd got himself quite a catch. I blushed, but was quite happy that he liked me. Jensen's dad told me his name was Anthony, but said that I could call him Tony as all his friends did. Tony was an art dealer and had moved back to Hove, from America, twenty-five years ago following his divorce from Jensen's mum, Sally. He explained that he and Sally were still good friends, despite getting divorced, and whenever he visited America he would often stay at Sally's house. I didn't know how Jensen's parents could do that, remain friends after their divorce! I didn't want to spend even one second in Sebastian's company once my divorce comes through. Mind you, if it works well for them then that's nice, and quite the grown up thing to do!

Tony showed me around his beautiful home, where a mix of old and new furniture adorned each room. He certainly had an eye for design, and knew which items of furniture blended well together. Huge paintings hung on every available wall space, and I was drawn to a painting of a beautiful lady, reclining on a chaise-longue, draped only in a sheet. 'I painted that one, many years ago. It's Sally, Jensen's mum.' He explained. Tony told me how he'd studied art at college when he was younger, and had ambitions of becoming an artist, but lost interest a few years after graduating. He went on to tell me that his passion for art had taken on a new direction, and that he had become an art dealer. 'I get a buzz out of being able to locate just the right pieces of art for those who wish to buy it. I've gained a good reputation for being able to get exactly what my clients are after.' He proudly declared. 'Some of the paintings that I've successfully purchased for my clients have been worth millions. I even managed to get hold of a Van Gogh for a rather well known actor.' He went on.

I asked him who the actor was but he confided that all his clients were guaranteed anonymity, so he couldn't divulge anything to me. 'I keep all my own paintings around the house though, the picture I painted of Sally was done when we first started courting, nearly thirty-five years ago, when Sally was just twenty-five! Tony then showed Jensen and I to his orangery, which was attached to one side of his house. It was adorned with plants, and in one corner stood a hot tub. I was quite surprised. When we entered the orangery, I thought it was Tony's garden room, but no, a hot tub sat, pride of place, in one corner of the room, with a bar in another corner. Tony saw the baffled look on my face and laughed out loud. 'Everyone I show this room to, has that same, puzzled expression on their faces.' He told me. 'I like to be different from everyone else, and this is my place of retreat when I feel stressed or overworked.' He explained. I sat at the bar and Tony served Jensen and I with a Pimms and lemonade each. We spent an enjoyable couple of hours in Tony's company, before making our way back to the hotel. I liked Tony, he was really nice and I sensed that Jensen was pleased that we'd got on well. After all, he was going to be part of my family once Jensen and I were married!

At the hotel I began to put my plan, of whisking Jensen away on a secret holiday, into action. 'Mum and dad are joining us for dinner tonight,' I told Jensen. 'And they're going to come and pick up the suitcases that I'd collected from Sebastian's house, and forward them on to us in New England.' I continued. Jensen thought that was a nice gesture! He still hadn't cottoned on, and didn't realise that I was going to sneak our holiday cases into my dad's car at the same time. I wasn't going to let Jensen in on my little secret until we reached the airport. I needed to settle the hotel bill without Jensen realising, as he'd told me that he was going to pay it, once our flights to America had been sorted out. 'I'll be two minutes.' I told Jensen, as I slipped out of the hotel room to pay a visit to reception to 'collect my messages', as I'd told Jensen! I settled my bill and returned to the our room, Jensen was sprawled on the bed, flicking through the television channels. I climbed onto the bed beside him and we sat and watched a film, We weren't due to meet my parents until 7 O'clock, so we spent an hour just laying around, relaxing like any other normal couple. Just after 7 O'clock my parents arrived. Jensen and my dad took the cases from Sebastian's, down to my dad's car. As they descended in one lift, my mother and I loaded the holiday suitcases into the other lift, so that we could secretly load them into dad's car too. Our timing had been perfect. As we reached the hotel lobby in our lift, Jensen had just taken the first lift back up to our room. Mother and I quickly passed the cases to my dad, and he loaded them into the boot of his car, then we all returned to the hotel lobby and summoned the lift to take us back up to our hotel room. As the lift doors opened, we were greeted by Jensen who'd been waiting patiently outside our locked, hotel room door. 'You'd forgotten my vanity case, and no girl can be without one of those!' I lied, as I unlocked the door to our room. 'Phew! I think I managed to get away with that one.' I thought to myself.

Bearing in mind that we needed to be at the airport in an hour and a half, I suggested that we should make our way to dinner. As we were dining in the hotel restaurant, we wouldn't have to spend time searching for a parking space, as we would have done, had we been eating out in the west end of London. Parking spaces there are like gold dust! I ordered a steak and salad, as did my mother, Jensen and my dad opted for trout. As it was relatively early the restaurant was fairly quiet, and the service quick, which was a good thing. We all ate our dinner rather quickly, my dad using the excuse that he had to pick some friends up from the airport soon. 'Anyone fancy coming for a ride, there's plenty of room?' My dad enquired. 'Yeah, we'd love to.' I replied, before Jensen could answer, and scupper my, so far, well executed plan.

My dad settled the restaurant bill, saying that it was his treat, before we headed off to the airport, with Jensen still none the wiser about the holiday! As luck would have it, the roads to the airport were quite clear and we arrived at the airport in plenty of time. My dad got out of the car and opened our door for us, then disappeared into the boot to retrieve our cases. I looked at Jensen. 'You and I are going on holiday! I told him 'I booked it as a surprise for you, and I enlisted the help of these two, to help me carry out my little scheme.' I announced, pointing at my mum and dad. To say Jensen was surprised was an understatement. Delighted, he picked me up, swung me round, and planted a big kiss on my lips. He shook dad's hand and kissed my mum on the cheek, and thanked them for getting us to the airport. I explained that mum and dad would fly to America with our cases, and Chloe's ashes, once we'd returned from our holiday. We picked up our cases and went off to find our check-in gate. Once we were checked in, and with our tickets in hand, we made our way to the departure lounge, and our boarding gate. We had time to sit and drink a coffee as we waited for our flight. Jensen was intrigued. He wanted to know how I'd managed to pull off his big surprise. I explained how I'd sneaked out of the hotel earlier that morning, while he'd been sleeping, and about my mad shopping frenzy to buy us both some holiday clothes. 'You never fail to amaze me. Thank you.' He said, as he leant over and kissed me. The airport was hectic, as ever, with people bustling about, trying to find out where they were supposed to be. We just sat holding hands and watched the world go by, contentedly waiting for our flight number to be called. It wasn't much longer before an announcement came over the Tannoy, inviting passengers to start making their way to the departure gate. We made our way towards the gate and joined the queue that had started to form. I'd booked us business class seats so we were allowed to board first. In the cabin there were huge, comfy, reclining leather seats, in rows of two, which meant that Jensen and I had a quiet corner of the plane together, where we wouldn't be disturbed. As we settled into our seats we were served champagne, and invited to peruse the evening's food menu to see what we might like to eat, by the flight attendant.

I wasn't really hungry as we'd not long eaten at the hotel. The attendant informed us that the meal wouldn't be served for about three hours anyway, so we made our selections. Jensen and I both opted for the chicken in white wine, served with seasonal vegetables, and a bottle of Champagne, as I wanted to toast my new life with Jensen. What better way to do it than sat in a plane, miles above the ground, miles from anywhere, eating wonderful food, and sharing a bottle of Champagne with the person you love sat next to you! We reclined our seats and settled down to watch the inflight movie that was showing. I must have been quite tired as I fell asleep. I was woken by the flight attendant who had arrived with our meals. I was surprisingly hungry and enjoyed every morsel that we were served. Once we'd finished our meals, Jensen and I reclined our seats into the 'bed' position and fell asleep once more, holding one another's hands. We were only woken by the captain's announcement that the plane was about to descend, and that we should put on our safety belts. I couldn't wait to start our holiday, nor could I wait to see the expression on Jensen's face when we arrived at our beach-front villa. I was going to be the first one in the outdoor whirlpool! We landed safely and were led to the exit door of the plane. We boarded the airport transfer bus which took us to the terminal building. We went through customs and immigration, through security, then to the baggage collection point and the baggage carousel. As luck would have it, our bags were amongst the first ones to come off the plane and arrived in the luggage collection area. Once we'd gathered our belongings we went outside, to board the sea-plane that was to take us to our holiday island! The weather was glorious. We could feel the heat of the early morning Sun already, radiating on our faces. The slight, cooling breeze was very welcome, but it wouldn't take us long to overheat if we weren't careful. We climbed aboard the sea-plane, and after a forty minute journey we arrived at our villa. It was in a small part of the island that was only open to only five beach-front villa's. It was certainly very quiet, and there'd be no need to dash to the beach early in a morning, to reserve a good sunbathing spot!

CHAPTER 9

The villa was furnished in a minimalist way, but the furnishings were of good quality. The kitchen had every appliance you could wish for and the bedroom had a huge, wooden four-poster bed, fitted with voile curtains to keep any insects that might get in, at bay. The bathroom was tiled from floor to ceiling with delicate blue and white tiles, although there was no bath, only a shower. We continued looking around the villa, Jensen opened the French doors which opened out onto the terrace, which overlooked the beach. In the corner of the terrace, was as expected, the outside whirlpool. 'Do you fancy joining me in there?' I asked Jensen, as I pointed towards the whirlpool, and without any hesitation Jensen started to strip off his clothes! The terrace was full of scented flowers and their petals, scattered around the whirlpool, filled the air with a heady scent. The water was warm and relaxing and the bubbles tickled in the naughtiest of places. I could feel the all my tension being drawn from my body, and for the first time in weeks, I started to truly relax.

We spent all morning in the whirlpool, relaxing, chilling out, and it was bliss. when we finally surfaced we looked like a pair of shrivelled prunes! We towelled each other down with the fluffy towels that had been left for us, got dressed, and took a walk along the beach. The sand was pure white and looked like a sea of diamonds as it shimmered in the Sun. It felt warm under our feet as we walked barefoot along the shoreline. The ocean was a coloured mixture of turquoise and blue, reflecting the sky above, and was crystal clear. I'd never seen such natural beauty before, it was like being in your own piece of heaven! The sky was cloudless, it was a perfect day, in a perfect setting. As we walked along the shoreline the waves splashed gently around our feet, cooling them after being heated by the warm sand. We could hear birds chirping in the trees that stood at the edge of the beach. The beach was completely empty and made everything even more magical. We had our very own private paradise! We were staying on South Nilandhoo atoll, Dhaalu Atoll, one of the islands of the Maldives. The group of islands measured only twenty-three kilometres by thirty-eight kilometres long. We were staying at the Vilu reef beach and spa, which was surrounded by natural vegetation and palm trees, and boasted a good range of water sports too. You could try your hand at windsurfing, waterskiing, scuba-diving or fishing, or you could take a trip on a Catamaran, even try out a kayak! The white sandy beach was surrounded by a coral reef and lagoon. There were three types of villa, a beach villa, a garden villa or a water villa. The beach and water villas were the more secluded of the villas, I had booked a beach villa. All the meals were served in the restaurant on the island, and was buffet style, whether it was breakfast, lunch, or dinner! It was an ideal honeymoon venue, but if you were looking for a retail therapy holiday, this definitely wasn't it! This was a place to get away from it all, a place where you could just be a couple without being disturbed or interrupted. There was no pressure on you to sample the activities on offer, if you preferred not to have a go it was your choice entirely.

Jensen and I thought that we'd book in for a massage and pamper ourselves a little, so I booked it for the following day. We were hungry, so Jensen and I decided to go and eat in the island's restaurant. We feasted on lobster, and seafood. You could definitely taste the difference between the freshly caught fish we had, and the fish you get in some of the restaurants in England. Once we'd eaten, we returned to our beach front villa and spent the next few hours sitting outside on the terrace, looking out over the ocean. It was so peaceful that it took us a while to get used to the silence. We both led busy lives and there was usually some form of background noise to be heard. Coming to a place like this, with the silence and peace it offered, was just indescribable. They say silence is golden, and this was no exception! I began to feel quite sleepy, I couldn't decide whether it was the sea air or the seven and a quarter hours it had taken for us to travel here on the plane, but I was certainly ready for my bed!

Jensen and I flopped onto our bed, we were so tired that we didn't even undress! I was even too tired to surprise Jensen with the new lingerie I'd bought in London, especially for this holiday! 'He'd just have to wait until tomorrow night when I'd give him a night to remember!' I thought, before drifting off to sleep. When we awoke the following morning, we found a platter, laden with fresh fruit, sitting on our table on the terrace. We ate the fruit for breakfast, then took an early morning swim in the ocean. It was a lovely way to start the day, and so invigorating! Once we'd finished our swim, we went for our massage. We were led onto the beach to a large gazebo. In the gazebo there were two beds, placed side by side. Two women, each dressed in a bikini and grass skirt came over to us, and began our massages, followed by our facials. Our pampering experience was topped off with a refreshing cucumber wrap. When I read about the cucumber wrap in the brochure, I thought it was something to eat, but it was actually a treatment where your body is wrapped in slices of cucumber. My body felt smooth, silky and hydrated. It was a wonderful experience, and one that I'd just have to sample again before our holiday was over!

Once we'd been pampered, we spent the afternoon on a boat trip that we'd booked. The boat was glass bottomed, and you could see all the different species of tropical fish that lived in the waters off the islands, and the different coloured coral reefs. It was like looking at a magical underwater kingdom, the turquoise blue of the ocean complimenting the various yellow striped fish. We were given the opportunity to take an underwater dive, to swim amongst the fish, and enjoy the true beauty of their underwater world. I liked swimming, but when it came to swimming alongside the various types of fish, I decided to give it a miss. I think some people are more at ease with that sort of experience then I am. I'd never fancied doing any of those types of water sport, Jensen told me that it wasn't his cup of tea either, but he'd enjoyed watching the fish, and seeing the coral reef through the glass bottom of the boat. Once we got ashore, we returned to our villa, as the Sun was very hot and we just needed to get into some shade. In the villa, the first thing Jensen did was turn on the air conditioning. We let the cool breeze waft against our skin to cool us down. We sipped some freshly squeezed orange juice, it glided effortlessly down my throat, cooling and lubricating the dryness away. I was surprised by how much more I needed to drink. I'd never realised just how much more fluid your body loses when in a hot country. I knew I needed to keep replenishing my body's water content, I just hadn't grasped how much fluid you lose through perspiration alone! We decided to go to the beach barbecue that the restaurant had organised, which was being held a little further down the beach from our villa. Having spent the afternoon touring the cool turquoise waters in a glass bottomed boat, we thought that we'd see what edible delights the beach barbecue would throw up. Jensen and I began to prepare for the evening's entertainment by taking a shower together. I chose to get showered with my favourite perfumed shower cream, Poison, by Christian Dior. I began to lather myself with the shower cream, covering every last part of my naked flesh. I'd promised myself that tonight Jensen would find out just how passionate he made me feel! The heady scent of the shower cream wafted around the steamy room, as Jensen stood behind me and began to massage my body with the cream. His hands glided easily over every inch of me, as if his hands were born to touch me, knowing every one of my erogenous zones. My body felt truly alive with the firm touch of his hands. I could feel his body pressing up against my back, his erect penis pushing up against my buttocks.

He began to kiss my neck with gentle, soft, kisses. His tongue traced a path to my shoulders, then Jensen began kissing me all over my back and down the tops of my legs. The water splashed against my skin, and Jensen's touch sent me into a sensual frenzy. Jensen spun me round so that I was facing him, and pulled me against his firm body. I kissed his masculine chest and teased his nipples with my tongue, letting my kisses follow a path to his stiff manhood. I began to tease and flick the end of his penis, hearing him gasp out loud with pleasure, as his bulbous, swollen tip twitched against my lips. Jensen took hold of my head and pulled me onto him, encouraging me to feed on him. I wasn't quite ready to go there yet, I wanted to tease him further, and hear him gasp and moan in pleasure some more. I licked the length of his erection, took his balls into my mouth, and gently sucked on them, sending Jensen wild with lust. He pulled me closer to his groin and began to gently gyrate against my face, begging me to take him in my mouth and taste him, which I now gladly did! Jensen's hands gripped my shoulders as I obeyed his command, and worked frantically with my mouth and tongue, to bring him off. With a final thrust of my mouth I took him deep, right to the back of my throat, where he came, with his final push. I swallowed his offering and licked my lips, before Jensen pulled me to my feet and knelt on the floor in front of me, parted my legs and started to tease my clit with his mouth, sucking my bud until he brought me to orgasm. His tongue probed my vagina, pushing deep inside me, darting in and out as he made love to me with his tongue. The intensity became too much and my legs began to shake as I exploded my juices all over his tongue. Jensen spun me round and bent me over so that he could take me from behind. My body was on fire and my head spun as Jensen started to glide his stiff, veiny cock deep inside me, back and forth, back and forth, building up speed and thrusting ever faster as my pussy gripped him firmly, only relaxing as he spurted his warm seed into me with a moan of pleasure. We held each other close for a few moments, then washed each other down. We stood in the shower for a short while, letting the water splash against our bodies. He cupped my face in his hands and kissed me. 'I love you with all my heart and I'm really looking forward to spending the rest of my life with you!' he told me, before kissing me gently on the lips.

I felt exactly the same! We emerged from the shower, and got ready for the barbecue. I put on a sundress that showed off my newly acquired tan and my heaving cleavage, just to tease Jensen some more! Jensen put on some shorts. He looked good in shorts, they showed off his powerful, muscular legs. He too had gained a nice tan and his body was bronzed and masculine. We arrived at the barbecue, where we got talking to a couple from Canada. They were on their honeymoon, they were called Kim and Steve. We all sat on the beach and tucked into our food. Steve and Kim seemed a nice enough couple, but every time Steve had something to say that was remotely funny, Kim would let out the most high pitched laugh, which made her sound a bit like a hyena! At the earliest opportunity, I told Jensen I didn't think that I could spend much longer in their company, as her high pitched laugh was beginning to give me a headache. It was some time later before we had the chance to make our excuses and leave their company, explaining that we really ought to mingle with the other guests too. There was a real variety of people on holiday, here on the island, and quite a few retired couples, enjoying their new found youth and spending more time together, now that their families had grown up, leaving them with time on their hands. We strolled along the beach. The sand was still warm from the heat of the day and it oozed between our toes as we searched for a nice quiet spot, where we could sit and watch the stars. It was so peaceful, our own little corner of paradise! The wind gently blew on our faces and the sky grew darker, as night began to fall, and the barbecue began to wind down as people made their way back to their villas! Except us! We wanted to sit and take in the breathtaking views. Just sitting here with Jensen reminded me of the time we sat on the beach together, in Brighton. Admittedly, the view here was better, and the weather warmer. I was however, still next to Jensen. I loved being close to Jensen, he gave me an inner peace that I'd never had, or felt before, and it felt magical! It's surprising how someone you spend time with, and share things with, can make you feel relaxed and content, and enable you to realise that feeling of inner peace, a feeling that we all have, but sometimes find hard to recognise. I think that finally I'd found what had been missing in my life. I'd finally filled the emptiness that I'd felt in my heart and it was all down to Jensen. Meeting him had enabled me to put things into perspective, and give me the strength, and the capability, to re-evaluate my life, and what in life was important to me. Jensen was my soul mate. When I started my journey of self discovery, trying to work out what I was to do about the situation I was in with Sebastian, I never envisaged such a drastic change. The whole process had been invigorating, surprising, and, at times heartbreaking, but it had made me a much stronger person, and I was glad. Jensen was good for me and I was never going to let him go!

By now the beach was empty, except for Jensen and I. Leaning my head on Jensen's shoulder, my eyes scanned his tanned body. Every time I looked at him my body would start to tingle. It was an instant reaction, every nerve in my body reacted to his presence, to his touch, and to the way his green eyes entranced me. He certainly had me under his spell! I kissed him gently as he held me close. This was the time I wanted to take him back to the villa and show him just how sexual he made me feel. I took him by the hand and led him back to our villa. Once inside the villa, I led him to the bedroom and told him to sit on the bed, whilst I got ready in the bathroom. He did as I asked as I slipped into the bathroom, to change into the lingerie I'd bought in London, especially for this holiday. I put on my fishnet stocking hold-ups, my black lace crotch less knickers, which encased my lips, and just barely showed my swollen and aroused clit. I slipped into my black satin maids dress, which displayed my cleavage and made my breasts look pert and full. I felt like Nell Gwynne offering up her wares! Finally, I stepped into a pair of black Stiletto's and picked up my prop, a feather duster. As I walked into the bedroom, Jensen's expression said it all. He certainly approved! Jensen stood up and beckoned me towards him. I did as I was asked. After all, I was his maid and I was ready and waiting to carry out his every wish. His lips pressed against mine as we kissed. He pushed my lips apart with his tongue and began to explore my mouth, his tongue was warm and probing. His hands encased my breasts as his mouth began to explore my neck and shoulders. My breath-ing became heavier as his hands slid over my satin dress. He pulled my dress up slightly, and cupped my mound with his hand. He gasped aloud as his fingers explored me. He realised that I was wearing crotch less knickers and I could tell from the way his shorts twitched that it pleased him. He gently prized my legs apart and started to rub my clitoris. I was in ecstasy, and began to get wet between my legs. The moistness of my pussy made Jensen's fingers glide easily along my smooth inner lips, and it wasn't long before he brought me to orgasm and drank my wetness.

I started to undress him and his clothes fell to the floor. He summoned me to kneel before his crotch. I gladly obliged, kissing his stomach and tracing a path towards his cock with my tongue. His cock began to grow longer as it swelled with excitement. He was bursting out of his boxers, so I slid them down his legs and onto the floor, where he stepped out of them. Jensen's bulbous end glistened with lubricant and I licked my lips in anticipation, at the thought of what he was going to ask me to do next. Jensen didn't ask me anything. He took my head, and pulled my mouth onto his member. His hands gripped my hair as he pulled me further onto him, and I began to 'deep-throat' him. Jensen lightly pulled at my hair as I slid my mouth along his shaft. Suddenly, he twitched, as I brought him to orgasm, into my waiting mouth. His seed dripped out of each side of my mouth, running down my chin and onto my breasts. He took his cock from my mouth, pulled me to my feet and began massaging his cum into my breasts. He picked me up and carried me over to the bed. As we lay down on the bed, I pushed him onto his back and straddled his thighs. I removed my stocking hold-ups, and tied his hands to the bedposts. I was in charge now, and it was my turn to be the dominant one. He had to do as he was told now! I took off my crotch less knickers and used them as a blindfold. Jensen's cock responded to my role playing. It was big and firm. He asked me what I was going to do to him. I told him not to speak, or I would have to 'punish' him. I licked his ears, and every now and then I'd slip my tongue into his ears and explore them, gently breathing into them at the same time, sending him into a frenzy. His body writhing and wriggling all over the bed as he tried to escape my restraints.

I took my feather duster and began to stroke it over his body. He groaned with pleasure! I was getting excited myself and clambered up towards his face. I hovered with my muff over his face and brought myself to orgasm, shooting my cum all over his face. Jensen demanded to be released. 'It's my turn to pleasure you!' He told me. I undid his restraints. Jensen positioned himself behind me and slowly, he slipped his penis inside me and began to make love. He pushed himself harder and deeper into me with each thrust. His hands wrapped around my waist as I cried out, as he fucked me ever faster. It felt as though he was trying to break me in two, but I wasn't complaining, his hard and fast lovemaking was wonderful. I felt dizzy, my body was tingling, and after a few more pushes of his penis, I orgasmed with such force, that I experienced 'Le petit mort', the little death! We both lay down, exhausted from our lovemaking session, and soon fell asleep.

When we awoke, we lay looking at each other. Jensen smiled at me. 'You were amazing!' I blushed, as I was slightly embarrassed, it was down to him that I'd become a raving nymphomaniac! Jensen told me that I should have been an actress, as my role playing was so believable. 'Who was acting?' I replied, and we both burst out laughing. How naughty were we? It was the last day of our holiday and although I was going to miss the island, I was looking forward to going back to New England. It was going to be a fresh start and I was looking forward to our future together. We both showered, and went to the restaurant to get a snack. Sex always made me hungry! In the restaurant the staff were just setting out the tables for breakfast. We shown to a small table on the terrace outside. The waiters explained that they would bring us over some coffee while they finished preparing the restaurant. Jensen asked me if I'd thought any more about our forthcoming wedding. He asked if we should set a date so that we could tell everyone, and start making arrangements. I said that I'd like to get married in his back garden with all our family and friends in attendance. Not that I had any friends left to invite, since marrying Sebastian! I'd lost touch with everyone, except Charlotte. I had acquaintances, people I'd met through Sebastian's work, but no one I could call a friend.

We discussed doing the garden up, with trellises, and trailing fresh flowers, and about holding the actual ceremony under an arbour. I could just picture it. It was going to be wonderful. We decided to set the date for three weeks time, which coincided with Jensen's birthday. I asked him if he minded sharing his birthday with our wedding day. He told me that it would be the best birthday present of all time. I made a mental note, to make sure Timothy had prepared all the relevant paperwork, so that I'd be officially divorced from Sebastian in time for me to marry Jensen. Finally, the waiter returned and invited us to make our way to the buffet table. It was more like a banquet than a buffet. There was a variety of freshly squeezed juices, a selection of fruit, cereals, bacon, eggs, you name it, everything you could think of was there.

Jensen helped himself to some bacon and toast, and I settled for orange juice and a bowl of cereal. Although I was hungry, I didn't want to overdo it on food, as we were flying back to America in a couple of hours time, and would be taking the seaplane to the airport. For some unknown reason, I felt nauseous flying in the seaplane, maybe it was because it was so small. You could feel the slightest of winds, which made the seaplane sway around and made me feel queasy. Once we'd eaten our breakfast, we returned to our villa to pack our suitcases. Luckily, there was just enough time for us both to have a final massage before leaving the island. We made our way to the outdoor massage area and had our tensions massaged away. We both emerged from the experience feeling relaxed, and eager to get on the plane home. I had really enjoyed our holiday, but was looking forward to getting to New England, so that I could put my wedding plans into action. Our departure time arrived and we boarded the seaplane. I think my massage had done me some good, as I wasn't the slightest bit nauseous on the journey back to the mainland. It had obviously been a bit of anxiety I'd suffered from on the outbound journey from the airport to the island. The airport terminal was quite quiet. Mind you, it was 8 O'clock in the morning! Perhaps the airport didn't get busier until the afternoon. We saw that a queue had formed ahead of us as we approached the check-in. 'Excuse me. Is this the queue for the flight to America?' I asked the lady at the end of the queue. 'Yeah, it sure is honey!' She bellowed, in a thick American accent.

We were soon through the check-in, but we had about an hour to kill, before our flight home. We bought a few newspapers to read, to help pass the time, and in what felt like no time at all we were being called to board our flight. We were on board, and on our way home! We snuggled back into our seats and put on our headphones, so that we could listen to some music. A stewardess came and asked us if we'd like a pillow and a blanket each, as we had a long flight ahead of us. We both accepted the offer and snuggled back into our seats once more. The plane taxied to the runway, before hurtling down it, the engines roared as the plane stepped up a gear, and were soon in the air, where we undid our safety belts and relaxed even further.

We were each given fresh fruit juice to drink and a pamper pack, which included things like eye masks, ear plugs, and wipes. I laid back, closed my eyes, and listened to the music playing through my headphones. I opened my eyes briefly, to see Jensen laughing, as I sang along to the music. I wasn't the best singer in the world, but I didn't think I was that bad! My thoughts took me back to the time I saw Jensen blasting out 'I Want to Break Free' in his kitchen! Jensen must have realised what I'd been thinking about. Maybe it was the big grin on my face that gave it away! We looked at one another and fell about laughing. We were a few hours into our flight when an air hostess came over and asked us to select our lunch from the menu.

Jensen chose duck, and I chose a Caesar salad, which was served to us shortly afterwards. After lunch we watched a movie. It was 'Meet the Fockers', the hilarious sequel to the film 'Meet the Parents' which I'd already seen. I liked comedies, and this film had me in stitches. It was about a young couple that had got together, and how they'd met one another's families. One family was portrayed as a normal, conventional family, and the other family were 'off the wall'. It showed a scene, where both families were seated together at the dining table, eating dinner, when the son's mother decides to get the family photo's out. She points out that their son had been circumcised as a boy, and promptly proceeds to produce the actual foreskin, which accidently falls into the cheese fondue! Perhaps it wasn't the ideal movie to play, after serving up food!

Once the film had finished we reclined our seats to make a bed, and covered ourselves with the blankets we'd been given. We still had a long flight ahead of us, so we decided to get some sleep. Just as we'd made ourselves comfortable, and ready to hit the land of nod, the air hostess brought us hot drinks and pastries, which we devoured before going to sleep. A few hours later we landed in America. It was night time and the airport was lit up like a firework display. It was raining pretty hard and as we made our way off the plane, to the shuttle bus which was waiting to take us to the terminal, we got soaked. We only had thin holiday clothes on and were not exactly dressed for wet weather! Even so I was glad to be home. The terminal was bustling, and busy as ever, in complete contrast to the island terminal where our journey had commenced.

Having collected our baggage, we made our way to the taxi rank, and within a few minutes a cab had picked us up to take us home. We eventually arrived at Jensen's house. The house was cold, as the heating hadn't been on for a few weeks. Jensen set about making a fire, and I went through to the kitchen, to find us something to drink. the milk in the fridge had, not surprisingly, turned sour. However, I managed to find some coffee whitener in one of the cupboards, so I put on a pot of coffee. We sat snuggled together on the sofa, wrapped tightly in the patchwork quilt I'd bought from the Amish village, but it wasn't long before the house had warmed up. It was nice to sit by the roaring log fire, sipping our coffee together. Jensen's answer-phone was flashing as he had some messages to retrieve. He played the messages. One message was from his mother, wondering why she hadn't heard from him, then there was a message from a couple of his friends, asking him to ring them, and a final message from someone enquiring about a price on a job. Jensen said he'd call everybody back the next day, as he wanted to spend the rest of the night with me, without interruption, that he wanted to make the most of the night, celebrating my return home with him. We sat and talked for most of the night, making plans for our wedding. Jensen said that he would ask Jake to be his best man, then we set about making a list of others we would invite to the wedding. We made a note to ring the local reverend, to see if we would be able to hold our wedding in Jensen's back garden, and there were the flowers to organise, our wedding outfits to buy, and plenty of other things besides. Jensen and I were going to visit his mother later on that evening. I hadn't met her before, I hoped she would like me, and not be too surprised by our forthcoming wedding. With all our lists finished and our coffee's drunk, we fell asleep on the sofa.

I didn't wake up until 10 O'clock the following morning. Jensen was already up and about. He was in the garden, building something out of wood. I went outside to see what he was up to. He turned and smiled as I called out to him. 'Good morning, sleepyhead!' He replied. 'I'm making a garden bench, the one I'd promised to make you for Chloe's memorial garden,' He took my hand and led me to one corner of the garden. 'and this patch of soil is where we're going to plant some flowers for Chloe.' He added. I was overcome with emotion, and tears welled in my eyes. 'Jensen you're so thoughtful.' I thought to myself, as I flung my arms tightly around him and gave him a kiss, to thank him. He had placed the wooden chair he'd bought for Chloe, next to the freshly dug soil. 'I thought it would be nice to have it here, as I'm gonna go and buy an angel statue to place between the garden bench and Chloe's chair.' He explained. I thought that was a lovely idea. 'I'll just finish the garden bench before we go to town.' He added. I went back into the house to take a shower and get ready.

I'd just finished getting ready when Jake tuned up. He was talking to Jensen and looked rather sad, so I went outside to see him. 'Hi Jake!' I called to him. Jake turned and gave me a hug. 'I'm sorry to hear about Chloe, Arabella. Is there anything I can do to help you, in making Chloe's memorial garden?' He asked. I asked him if he knew of anywhere I could get an angel statue from. Jake told me that he knew just the place. 'I can take you there now, if you like.' I looked at Jensen, who told me to go ahead. 'It'll give me time to finish the bench.' He said, with a smile. I collected my jacket from the house and climbed into Jake's Jeep. Jake congratulated Jensen and I, on our impending wedding, telling us that he would be honoured to be Jensen's best man.

As we travelled, I told Jake that I needed his help with a surprise wedding gift that I wanted to get Jensen, to which he agreed. Jake took me to an old, ramshackle, house. It was where an old man lived, who was well known in the area for his stonework and woodcarving. Jake explained to the man what I was looking for. The old gent invited us into his workshop and showed us his statues. In one corner of the room, stood the most beautiful angel statue that I'd ever seen. It was an angel with her wings draped around a little girl. 'THAT is the statue I want!' I told the man, and agreed a price, while Jake loaded the statue into his Jeep. On the way home Jake asked what I needed his help with, regarding Jensen's wedding gift. I explained that I wanted to find out who owned the field behind Jensen's house, as I wanted to buy it for Jensen. I wanted to erect a big barn on the land, for

Jensen to use as a workshop and salesroom for his carpentry. I explained how I wanted to set Jensen up with his own business, instead of him working for others. I knew that he hadn't worked for a few weeks as he'd been over in England, supporting me in my hour of need. I wanted to repay his kindness by giving him stability through owning his own business, and not having to rely on others employing him. Jake thought it was a great idea, and told me that he knew who owned the land, and would take me straight to their house, to see if I could persuade them to sell their field to me. the couple who owned the land weren't really looking to sell, but after a little persuasion, and the generous offer I made them, they found the opportunity to sell too good to miss. I wrote out a cheque for the agreed price, including the cost of erecting a new barn, which they'd agreed to build for me, and with a handshake, the job was done, I had just bought Jensen some land!

I told Jake it was going to be a secret wedding gift and not to let Jensen know what I'd done, to which he agreed. We made our way back to Jensen's house, or should I say our house, and when we arrived, Jensen had finished the garden bench. It was lovely, a nice piece of craftsmanship. Jake placed the angel statue in the garden, next to the bench, and we all went inside for a glass of homemade lemonade, as the weather was getting quite hot. I rang Timothy to see if the legal paperwork had been done. He told me that he'd pulled in a few favours, and as of lunchtime, I was officially divorced. He was going to 'Fed-Ex' the papers to me straight away. I was finally free, and I cheered out, loudly. Jensen and Jake came into the room to see what I was cheering out loud about, I told them that I'd tell them later. Jake explained that he had some errands to run, and would have to go.

On his way out of the door, Jake asked if we wanted to meet up in the pub, for a celebratory drink later on, to which we agreed. Jensen tried his mothers phone number but there was no answer, so he left a message for her to call him. We rang the local reverend who arranged to meet us the next day, to discuss our arrangements. Jensen disappeared into the bathroom to take a shower, as he was full of sawdust and mud. When he emerged from the shower I told him the good news, that I was now officially a free woman, and free to marry him. Jensen was delighted at the news, and suggested we go into town to pick our wedding rings. I didn't need inviting twice, and raced to Jensen's truck, climbed into the cab, and sat there with an huge grin on my face. I was so happy. Jensen locked up the house then climbed into his truck beside me, and we drove off to town.

CHAPTER 10

We arrived in town, where we stopped off at a small jewellery shop. There were loads of rings to choose from, but in the end we picked out two Platinum wedding bands, one for me and one for Jensen. 'I'd like something special engraved on the inside of my husband's wedding band. It's to be a surprise!' I told the sales manager, in a whisper so that Jensen couldn't hear. The sales manager invited me to follow him. We went through a curtain, into a little room beyond. It was the room where he carried out his repairs and engraving. 'Now what would you like engraving?' he asked, to which I replied, 'Jensen, my soul provider, with love, Arabella.' I walked back through the main room of the shop, where Jensen was patiently waiting for me. We collected our rings, and I made my way to the bridal shop whilst Jensen headed off to the menswear shop. I had no idea what kind of wedding dress to choose. All I knew was that I wanted something in ivory!

There were hundreds of different dresses and styles to choose from and I must have tried on at least a dozen, but I still couldn't find one that I thought was right. I was about to give up hope when, out of the corner of my eye, I spotted the most beautiful dress. I just hoped that it was in my size! I walked over to the rail where it hung and picked it up. 'Yes!' I thought, as I checked the label. 'It's my size. Now, let's see how it looks on me. the dress was all in ivory, just as I wanted, but with a burgundy bodice. It fitted me perfectly. It was the dress I had to have! I took it to the sales counter, paid for it, and told the shop assistant that I'd collect it in a couple of weeks time. I left the bridal shop and went in search of Jensen, to see if he'd managed to find a suit to wear for our big day. He had, but he didn't want me to see it. 'You can't see it. It's a surprise, just like your wedding dress, you'll see it on our wedding day, and not before! He said, jokingly. Jensen too, had arranged to collect his suit in a couple of weeks time. we decided to go for a coffee, so that we could sit and see what else on our list we needed to organise. We still had the flowers, the caterer, and the Reverend to sort out. Once we'd finished our drinks we walked on, to the flower shop, where we chose some dark red Dog roses to go in my bouquet. We also chose the same flowers to go round the ceremonial arbour, in our garden. We arranged for the flowers to be delivered on the morning of the wedding, the florist explained that they would decorate the arbour then. With the flowers organised, we made our way to the caterers. We weren't sure of the kind of food we wanted for the wedding. We didn't know whether to pick buffet style, or a sit down meal. If we had a sit down meal, then we would need to organise the marquee, tables and chairs for the guests. The caterer was really nice, she showed us the different menu styles, and the options available. I had to admit, she was very patient with us, but in the end we chose a simple menu. I didn't want anything fancy, nor did I want 'posh' food like Canapés, I just wanted 'normal' food that everyone liked. We opted to serve platters of freshly caught seafood and fish, platters of cooked meat, quiche and other savouries. Platters of ribs and chicken, platters of fresh fruit, and bowls of potato, and mixed salad. Everybody liked that kind of food, so we knew it would all be eaten!

The caterer told us that she would also make us a cake, and, as neither Jensen or I were fond of fruit cake we opted for a simple sponge cake, decorated with royal icing and flowers. Once we were happy with our choice of wedding menu, and the type of food we'd chosen we paid the caterer and left the shop. We only had the Reverend left to see. Jensen had previously spoken to him on the telephone, and he'd said that there shouldn't be a problem with holding the wedding at our home, and that he was available to marry us on Jensen's birthday. It was just a case of finalising which songs were to be played, and whether we wanted to say the traditional vows to each other, or use our own vows. We were due at the Reverend's house at four-thirty, half-an-hour's time, just enough time for us to grab a coffee in the little tea-room nearby! We ordered our coffees and two sandwiches. We'd covered quite a lot of the wedding preparation and I was quite pleased with the progress we'd made. Planning our wedding had been a pleasure, and I couldn't wait for the day to come. The day I marry Jensen! We finished off our food and set off to meet the Reverend. He wasn't what I'd expected, and although I didn't have any preconceptions, other than he would be like the vicar I had back in England, I was way off the mark!! The Reverend was a thirty-something biker who was down to earth. I liked him. He wasn't your usual 'stuffed shirt', but rather a hip and trendy Reverend, and I warmed to him straight away. We told him that we wanted to say the traditional vows to each other, but not have traditional church music played. Instead I wanted the song that was playing in the restaurant, when Jensen proposed to me, and we wanted 'our' song to play when we said our vows. We wanted Michael Bolton's 'The Best of Love' and Aerosmith's 'I Don't Want to Miss a Thing'. We made arrangements to get married at 3 O'clock, which would give everybody time to prepare the flowers in the garden, and the food. We'd completed our list of to do's, we just had to try and ring everyone and tell them the date and time of our wedding, so they could make their travel arrangements to get to our wedding.

My parents were due to fly in from England in a few days time, so they'd be here for the wedding. We still had to get hold of Sally, Jensen's mum, and also Tony, Jensen's dad. We headed off home to make our phone calls, and to get ready to go out, as we were due to meet Jake later, in the local pub. At home, the red light on the answer-phone was flashing again, which meant that we had some messages. There were two messages, one from Sally, saying that she was going to be popping over at six this evening. 'Oh my God, that's only twenty minutes away! I'd better make myself look presentable.' I thought. The other phone call was from Jake, to say that he would be in the pub at seven-thirty with the rest of the gang. I quickly showered and put on my little black dress. I wanted to make a good impression on Sally, and I thought if I got dressed up she would see that I wasn't a slob. that I was worthy of marrying her son. The only thing that worried me, was how Sally felt about our age difference! Jensen told me not to panic, as his mum had a similar personality to his dad, and I'd got on well with his dad when we met, so there was nothing to worry about!

At five-to-six there was a knock at the door, it was Jensen's mum. Jensen invited her in and said that he wanted to introduce her to someone special. Me! I said 'Hello' and Jensen introduced me to her as his Fiancée. 'When did this happen?' She enquired. She asked how long we had been together. 'Just over three and a half months.' Jensen declared. We sat down and talked for a while, getting to know each other, and despite Sally's initial shock at meeting her son's fiancée, and soon to be, wife, we got on really well together. Sally said that she was glad that her son was finally going to settle down, and would love to be a part of our wedding. The relief must have shown on my face, as she gave me a hug and welcomed me to the family. We invited her along to the pub for a celebratory drink, but she said she had other plans as she'd got a new man in her life, and they were going on their first date. We arranged to meet her in a couple of days time, at her house, and off she went to have her first date with her new man! We phoned Tony and gave him the news of our forthcoming marriage. He was delighted, and told us that he'd sort out his travel arrangements. Things were coming together just fine!

I made Jensen a cuppa, and we sat on the sofa, reflecting on the day's events. I told him that he had made me the happiest woman on Earth. He smiled, and playfully squeezed my knee. Jensen decided to take a shower, so I took the opportunity to ring the man who I'd bought the field off, to see when he intended to start building the barn, as I wanted it to be finished in time for the wedding. 'I'll be starting work on it in the morning my dear.' The man told me. I thanked him and quickly put down the phone, as Jensen appeared in the room, looking and smelling heavenly. 'You ready sexy?' He asked, with a cheeky smile. 'I'm always ready!' I teasingly replied, and with that we locked the door of the house, and we set off for the pub to meet up with Jake, Toby, Melissa, and Heather.

The pub was full when we arrived. We spotted Melissa and Toby near the dartboard. We made our way over to them, where everyone congratulated us and generally made a fuss over us. Melissa asked if I'd planned to have any bridesmaids at my wedding. I hadn't thought of that, and I didn't have anyone that

I could ask. Heather said that she and Melissa would love to step in, and take the role of bridesmaids, if I liked. 'Ooh! Yes please!' I answered, and we made arrangements to meet at the bridal shop the following morning, to buy their bridesmaids dresses. The night passed really quickly, and I'd managed to stay relatively sober, unlike the previous time we'd all met up! It was Jensen who was worse for wear this time. everyone had insisted on buying him drinks to celebrate our wedding, and he'd been too polite to refuse. I'd never seen Jensen drunk before. He wasn't a bad tempered person when he'd had too much to drink, as some can be, but a romantic, quite cute guy, who insisted on declaring his undying love for me, to anyone who would listen! Toby offered us a lift home, and Jake said that he would follow us in Jensen's truck. Outside the pub Jake, Toby and I all helped to put Jensen into Toby's truck. 'I don't envy you and the big headache you'll have in the morning!' I thought, as I looked at Jensen, lolling unsteadily in the passenger seat of Toby's truck. I didn't mind though, it just meant that I'd have to play nursemaid to him. 'Mmm, that's something to consider in our love games!' I thought to myself.

We arrived home and managed to put Jensen to bed, and within minutes he was fast asleep. I thanked the boys for their help, and bid them goodnight, before closing the door. I tidied round a little, before making myself a hot chocolate. I didn't make one for Jensen, there was no point, he was deep in the land of nod! I drank my chocolate and locked up, before undressing and slipping into bed next to Jensen, and snuggling up to his back. Jensen was oblivious to the fact that I was cuddled up next to him but I didn't mind, my knowing that I was next to him was all I needed. Jensen began to snore, and I soon fell asleep as I listened to the rhythmic snoring sounds he made.

The Sun shone brightly through the open curtains the next morning, and I could hear the birds singing in the trees outside, the sky was clear and a beautiful blue. It was a glorious day! I got up and went into the kitchen to make Jensen some breakfast. I didn't want to make him anything too heavy, as his stomach probably wouldn't appreciate it. I made him some scrambled eggs and muffins, and a mug of hot coffee. I put them on a tray, along with a glass of water and two headache tablets. I put the tray down on the bedside table and whispered gently in Jensen's ear. 'Jensen, wake up.' He sat up in bed, a little worse for wear. He was thankful for the painkillers! Jensen managed to eat some of his breakfast, but as he tried to get out of bed, he felt dizzy. I helped him back into bed and told him that he had to stay put, as I was going to look after him for the rest of the day. I opened the bedroom window to let in some fresh air, before bringing him a wet facecloth and placing it on his forehead. I climbed into bed beside him and stroked his hair until he fell asleep. Once he was asleep, I went into the kitchen to make a broth. Whenever Chloe or Sebastian had been ill I made them some broth, and it always seemed to make them feel better. I hoped that it would have the same, desired effect on Jensen. I peered out of the kitchen window, and noticed that the frame of the barn, in the adjoining field, had already been erected. It wouldn't be long before it would be finished completely. The phone rang, it was Jake checking to see how Jensen was. I told him that he was resting in bed, so Jake said that he'd phone him later. I decided that my next job was to sort out the spare bedroom as my parents were due in tomorrow, and they were going to stay with us. I rang them to make sure that they were still coming. They had to be at the airport by 9 O'clock this evening, for check-in. My dad told me that everything was on schedule, and not to worry. He told me that he'd collected Chloe's ashes, and would be bringing them over. I told him about the memorial garden Jensen had created, to which my dad replied, 'I'm pleased that you've found such a caring, selfless man.' I told him about our wedding, on Jensen's birthday, and dad said that they would extend their stay with us, so that they wouldn't miss it. I bid my dad goodbye and put down the receiver. As I did so, I heard Jensen call out to me. He asked me to take him a glass of water, as he still wasn't feeling too good. I gave him a glass of water and a bowl of my broth, with strict instructions to eat it all, as it would make him feel a lot better. Jensen did as he was told, and ate the broth. He turned to me and apologised for being ill. I told him that he didn't have to apologise, as he couldn't help feeling poorly, and that it was my turn to look after him, as he'd looked after me in the past. Jensen gave me a smile, and fell back to sleep. After a few hours had passed, Jensen emerged from the bedroom looking a lot better. 'I'm going outside to finish off Chloe's memorial garden, before your mum and dad arrive tomorrow.' He explained. 'Anyway, the fresh air might do me some good!' He added. We'd planned to hold our memorial service with my parents in attendance. Eventually, Jensen called me into the garden to see what he had done. It was a beautiful creation. He'd planted flowers all around the garden bench he'd made, and around the chair he'd bought for Chloe. I flung my arms around his neck. I couldn't speak as I was choking back the tears, Jensen had done me proud! We walked back into the house and just lounged about on the sofa for the rest of the evening. I kept wondering what my parents would make of Jensen's efforts. I was sure they'd have plenty of favourable comments to make. The following day we picked up my parents from the airport, and headed back to our house. My dad was very impressed with Jensen's home, especially with the items of furniture that Jensen had made. My mother was quite taken with the garden. She liked gardens, in fact I think she would be happy just living in a garden shed, as long as the garden was perfect. My parents were delighted with Jensen's efforts, and what he'd done with the memorial garden for Chloe, and as the night drew in we all went into the garden with our candles and said a prayer as we stood round the angel statue, and buried Chloe's ashes. It was a simple but very emotional send off, Chloe was now here with us, and could now watch over us all.

We went back inside to get ready to meet Sally, Jensen's mum. We were going over to her house, to introduce my parents and to get to know each other a little better. Sally's house was the total opposite to Tony's, it was small, but every available space was filled with pictures, and artists materials. She, like Tony, was a very talented artist, and she painted the most beautiful flower, and landscape pictures that I'd ever seen. I was quite taken with a painting of an Iris that she had painted. Sally insisted that we had it as an engagement present! The night went well, it was very informal and there were no airs and graces, even from my mother! I saw my mother in a very different light, she had become much more calm, more at ease than I had ever seen her before. My parents got on well with Sally, and she too, with them. Sally's house was filled with laughter and it had been a lovely evening all round. My mother and Sally arranged to meet up the next day, and go out to choose their wedding outfits together, while my dad and Jensen were going to go and choose a suit for my dad, and the best man. I was supposed to be meeting up with Heather and Melissa, to get their bridesmaids dresses, but Heather had to work late, so she and Melissa had rung the bridal shop and arranged to go after work, so I was going to meet them at the shop. We drove home in Jensen's truck, it was after midnight when we got in, so we bid each other goodnight and made our way to our rooms. I woke early so that I could prepare breakfast for us all. I made a huge plateful of pancakes, bacon, and eggs. Jensen joined me in the kitchen to make a pot of coffee, and a few minutes later we were joined by my parents, who'd arrived for their breakfast. After breakfast we all went our separate ways, to finish off our wedding shopping. I had to go to the florists to order some more posies for my bridesmaids to carry. I also wanted to check on the progress of the barn I was having built for Jensen, and organise a sign for his new business. Jake told me about one of his friends who was a sign-writer, so I'd arranged for Jake's friend to come down to the house while everyone was out. The barn was beginning to take shape, the roof and the sides were being erected, as I looked on. The old man had promised me that the barn would be finished by the following day as he'd employed a few of the locals to help him with the build, to speed up the process. They certainly had worked very hard!

It was teatime by the time Jensen returned from town with my parents. I just had time to say 'Hello', before leaving to meet up with Heather and Melissa at the bridal shop. Jensen said that he would do a barbecue for when I got back, and that he had invited Jake, Toby, Melissa, and Heather over. I gave him a quick 'peck' on the lips and set off for the dress shop. Melissa and Heather were already at the bridal shop, trying on dresses. Eventually we all decided that the best option would be to go for burgundy bridesmaids dresses with a fitted bodice. They both looked lovely, and I couldn't help smiling to myself, as my wedding was coming together nicely.

Back at the house the barbecue was in full swing. My dad was serving the wines and beers to everyone, while my mother was busy in the kitchen making lots of different side salads, and marinating the chicken for the barbecue. I had been quite impressed with my mother over the last couple of days, she seemed to have climbed down from her pedestal, and was making a conscious effort to get along with people. I would even go as far as to say that I think she was starting to really enjoy herself! The evening went brilliantly, everyone had enjoyed it so much that nobody wanted to go home, so we ended up with Jake, Toby, Melissa, and Heather, crashing out on the lounge floor! At the barbecue Jensen had mentioned to Jake that there was a new barn being built on the field next door, and he wondered who had bought it. If he only knew!! I hoped that I could keep that a secret until our wedding day. I wasn't exactly great at keeping secrets, good secrets that is. I knew he would be shocked, and pleased at the same time though, once I revealed my wedding gift to him, on our wedding day. The following morning brought quite a few sore heads, and most of us could only manage a cup of coffee. My mum had risen from her bed bright and early, to cook us all breakfast. I was sure she had an iron stomach, she'd drunk more than I had, yet it was me who was suffering, not her! I suppose it had been all the years she'd spent entertaining her friends that had given her the iron stomach. Eventually our guests found the strength to get up and go to their own houses, while Jensen and I went back to bed to recuperate. My parents decided that they'd do a bit of sight-seeing and had organised a hire car for a week. They planned to go and explore the area, and were going to book into a different hotel each night, as they travelled from place to place. They said that they would be back in plenty of time for the wedding, which was now only two weeks away!

Jensen and I spent the next week together, doing our own thing. It was nice to be able to spend time together, just the two of us. We went to the hotel that Jensen and I stayed in, the night he proposed to me. We booked it for the few days after our wedding, as a honeymoon. I didn't want to go anywhere exotic, after all we had only recently arrived home from the Maldives. We both wanted to book somewhere special for our honeymoon, and this hotel was special. It was where we had promised ourselves to one another for ever. Over the next few days, Jensen had to go to work. He was trying to get done all the jobs that he'd arranged to do, before our wedding, so he could take some time off once we were married. He had postponed some of the jobs that he was due to do so that he could come and be with me in England, so the work he was currently dealing with, couldn't wait any longer. My parents had extended their car hire, as they were having a whale of a time exploring New England, but promised to be back the day before we were due to get married, which, I might add, had come round rather quickly!! I was getting married to Jensen in three days time and I couldn't wait. I'd heard that Tony had flown in from London, and was staying at Sally's. The barn was finished, and all the new machinery that I'd bought, with Toby's help, had been installed. The shop sign was going to go up the night before our wedding, so as not to let Jensen find out about his surprise. I'd been quite impressed with Jensen's friends, and the way they had, and indeed were, helping me to organise the surprise. They thought that Jensen would be thrilled at having somewhere of his own to run his business from, instead of running it from home. It was the least I could do for him, especially as he had done so much for me I felt equal to Jensen, we both helped each other with life and its problems, and we truly loved each other. This was a marriage that was going to last, I was sure of it, I could feel it in my soul.

It was the day before our wedding, and my parents had returned to our house. The owner of the flower shop had called by to oversee the erection, and floral decoration of the arbour, and the caterer had arrived, and was busy setting out the tables and chairs under the marquee. She dressed each table with tablecloths and napkins, and adorned each table with fresh flowers. The dresses had been delivered, as had the suits, and everything was coming together nicely. My dad and Jensen were busy practising their speeches, whilst my mother and I had our nails done in the local beauty salon. We'd arranged for the hairdresser to come to the house on the wedding morning. Tonight, Jensen was going to stay at his mum's house, as he wanted to do things properly! He told me that he couldn't wait to see me tomorrow, and was looking forward to seeing me standing beside him in my wedding dress in the afternoon. I was going to miss him tonight, and even though I knew that he was only going to be gone for one night, even that seemed like a lifetime. I gave Jensen his birthday present before he left for his mother's house. I'd bought him a new truck, and had arranged for Jake to bring it over from his house whilst Jensen was packing his overnight bag and getting his wedding suit together. Jensen couldn't believe his eyes, when I led him outside to see his birthday present. He had needed a new truck, as his old truck was at least ten years old and had started to show its age. It was in need of a lot of work! I'd had Jensen's name, and business sign-written on each side of his new truck. He was so shocked at his present that all he could do was stand there with his mouth wide open, as his eyes surveyed his new truck! Jensen picked me up and spun me round as he kissed me. I think he was pleased! He kept telling me that I shouldn't have spent all that money, that just being with him was all he wanted. I jokingly said that I had better send the truck back if he didn't want it, and he said course he wanted it, he loved it, but he didn't expect me to spend so much on his birthday present. I told him he deserved a treat, and anyway I was happy to spend what I had on him. He kissed me goodbye. He had such an effect on me, that I had tears in my eyes as I didn't want to let him go, even for one night! I was going to miss him, miss cuddling up next to his body in bed, and miss the safeness of his arms around me, even though I knew he would only be gone for one night, that was one night too many! Jensen wiped away my tears and told me that he loved me. By now he was getting emotional too. We held on to one another's hands as he climbed into his new truck, and with a final kiss, we said our goodbyes, at least until tomorrow.

I walked into the house and went straight to bed. The bed seemed huge without Jensen next to me. I had gotten used to him lying next to me, hearing his gentle breathing, as he slept next to me, and feeling his touch when we made love. 'No,' I thought, 'This isn't a feeling I'll get used to!' I must, eventually, have drifted off to sleep. I was awoken the next morning by my mother, with a cup of tea. The hairdresser was due in an hour, so I had to get up and get dressed. I took a shower to wake myself up properly. I was still tired, as I'd only managed to get four hours sleep. I put on a pair of jogging bottoms and a tee-shirt, I was going to be busy all morning, I was having my hair and make-up done, the caterers would be delivering the food, and the posies and bouquets would be arriving, so there was no point in getting dressed up, as I had a lot to sort out. Melissa and Heather arrived to get their make-up and hair done. I told my mother that she, Heather and Melissa should have their hair and make-up done first, as I had a few things still to do. I wanted everything to be perfect for our wedding and the only guarantee I had of that, in my mind, was for me to oversee all the jobs that still needed sorting myself. The flowers arrived first, followed not long after, by the caterer and their wares. The food looked lovely. Simple, but delicious, and it was presented so beautifully. I took a stroll over to Jensen's barn, to see if the sign had been put up the night before, as I'd asked, and there it was, just as the old man had promised me. It was nice to know you could still trust some folk to keep their word! I walked into the barn to see how it looked inside. It was the first chance I'd had to view the finished product, and I wasn't disappointed. The barn interior had been laid out in different zones. There was a reception area, where Jensen could meet and greet his customers, a shop where all his furniture could be displayed, and from where he could sell it, and finally, a large workshop to the rear of the barn, with all the latest woodworking machinery, lathes, drills, and a thickness planer, to name but a few tools, indeed there was everything the carpenter about town could wish for! I'd also bought Jensen some new hand tools, as I knew that he preferred to make his furniture using the traditional methods. The woodworking machinery would come in handy if he secured large orders that needed completing in a short space of time. I was delighted with the barn, and was sure Jensen would really love his barn too. My inspection over, I headed back to the house to have my hair and make-up done, satisfied that all the jobs had been done. As I entered the house, my mother was on the phone. She was talking to Jensen, who was ringing to tell me that he loved me, and asking if I still wanted to marry him.

My mother handed me the phone. 'Of course I still want to marry you!' I told him. 'You're not having second thoughts?' I asked. Jensen laughed, 'I thought you might have changed your mind. I still find it hard to believe that someone as beautiful and caring as you, would want me.' he told me I'd always want him, and he replied that the feeling was mutual, he'd always want me. Jensen told me that he'd left a little present for me in the top drawer of his bedside table. I bid Jensen goodbye, put down the phone, and ran through to the bedroom. Opening the drawer, I saw a red box. I took the box from the drawer and opened it. I gazed in awe at the beautiful contents. The box contained a pair of diamond earrings, and a diamond necklace.

There was a note enclosed in the box which explained that he'd bought them for me to wear with my wedding dress. The crafty devil had bought them at the jewellers while I'd been getting the engraving done on his wedding band! I was lost for words. He was such a thoughtful man, I really loved him and couldn't wait to become his wife. I dashed to the phone, and called Jensen at his mother's house. 'Oh Jensen, I love you so much! Thank you! The necklace and earrings are beautiful. I can't wait to see you.' I gushed, I was so happy. I was feeling really emotional, and just wanted some time to myself. I went into the garden, and sat on the garden bench, in Chloe's memorial garden, and started to talk to Chloe. I wished that she could have been here, to be part of my special day. I told her that I was sure she would have loved Jensen, like I did. It would have been nice to have seen her in a cute little bridesmaids dress. I hoped that Chloe was looking down from heaven, watching me getting married to someone who made me feel loved and wanted, marrying someone who made me happy! I glanced up to the sky and whispered to Chloe to send me a sign, if she was watching over me on this special day.

My thoughts were interrupted by the hairdresser, screaming at me. 'Come inside and have your hair and make-up done!' I ran inside to get ready. Once my hair and make-up was done, I put on my wedding dress. I'd just finished fastening it up as my dad walked into the room. 'Arabella, you look absolutely stunning!' He told me, as tears welled in his eyes. 'Ooh, don't set me off,' I cried. 'or my make-up will run.' My dad kissed me on the cheek and said that he knew that I was doing the right thing. He could tell by the way Jensen and I acted when we were with each other.

Suddenly my mother came rushing into the room. 'Jensen and the other guests have just arrived, and the Reverend is waiting for your dad to walk you into the garden, to stand at Jensen's side.' She declared. The CD with our wedding tunes began to play. 'Well here we go.' I thought. 'It's time to marry the man of my dreams.' As I walked to the front of the arbour to be at his side, Jensen turned round and smiled. 'I love you!' He whispered. Jensen looked gorgeous in his suit, very handsome indeed! We both said our vows to each other, and the Reverend pronounced us man and wife. It was official, I was Jensen's wife! Everyone sat under the marquee, eating and drinking. When it was time for the wedding speeches, my dad stood up and told everyone how proud he was that he had such a lovely son as Jensen, how pleased he was that we had married, and that it made him happy to see his daughter with a smile on her face once more. My dad sat down, and Jensen rose to his feet. He spoke about the first time we met, as we'd travelled on the plane over to America. 'I knew from the very first moment we met, that Arabella would be forever in my life. I'd hoped to have Chloe in my life too, to complete my family, unfortunately it wasn't to be, and although Chloe and I never got to speak, I sense her presence whenever I'm with her mum. I'm sure Chloe would have given me her blessing, had I been able to ask if I could be her new daddy, and I'm sure, today, she would have looked just as beautiful as her mum does!' Jensen told the guests, as he looked down, towards me.

We both smiled at one another, we had matching, tear-filled eyes, and so did the guests. Indeed there wasn't a dry eye in the place, as everyone choked back their tears. Jensen's speech had been beautiful and heartfelt, and as I looked towards him, out of the corner of my eye, I saw the sky light up as a rainbow appeared. I felt such a powerful, warm glow inside me, and knew, at that precise moment, that it was a sign from Chloe in the heavens above, giving us her blessing, letting us know that she was watching over us all as we celebrated. With the speeches and the first dance out of the way, I pulled Jensen aside. I wanted to show him my wedding present to him. I asked him to follow me, as we walked across the adjacent field to the barn. Jensen asked me where we were going, and I told him not to be so impatient, that all would shortly be revealed! As we approached the front of the barn I asked Jensen to close his eyes, just until we reached the barn doors. Reluctantly Jensen agreed. Arriving at the front of the barn, I told him that he could open his eyes. Jensen looked up at the sign above the doors, and with a confused expression asked why the barn had his name above the doors. When I told him what I'd done, and showed him round the barn, he was lost for words, and didn't know what to say. 'Are you pleased?' I asked. Jensen took my hand and turned to me. 'You never stop surprising me Arabella, how did you manage to pull this one off?' He enquired. I explained how Jake and Toby had helped me to keep my little secret a surprise. 'I'm overwhelmed, lost for words. To think that anyone would do such a wonderful thing as this for me. Thank you so much! I'll make you really proud. This business will be a success, and I'll make sure you have everything in life that you could ever want.' He declared. Little did he know, but he'd already given me everything in life I wanted, himself, when he made his vows to me! We spent a little while longer in the barn, before heading back to the party. The party was in full swing when we got back. Tony had even managed to get my mother up for a dance, whilst Sally and my father were deep in conversation with Heather and Melissa. We thanked everyone for coming to our wedding, and told them to continue partying, as we were heading off to our honeymoon at the hotel.

My mum and dad were going to look after our house while we were staying at the hotel, they were going to fly back to England in a few days time. We packed enough clothing to last us, and I included some sexy lingerie. We changed out of our wedding clothes and set off for the hotel to start our honeymoon. We'd booked into the very same room that we stayed in previously. In the room there were fresh flowers on a small table by the window, and a bottle of Champagne and two glasses waiting for us. The bed was covered in red rose petals, there were lit candles on the bedside tables, and a huge basket of fruit, and a box of the finest Belgian chocolates sat on the dressing table. It looked so romantic! In the bathroom there were two fluffy bathrobes and a selection of luxury toiletries. The hotel really had made an effort to make things just perfect for our special day. Jensen poured me a glass of Champagne and we toasted our new life together. I was going to enjoy being married to Jensen. Jensen asked me if I wanted to share a bath with him. I nodded that I would. How could I resist? Jensen walked into the bathroom and began to run our bath.

'Arabella, bath's run!' Jensen called out, after about five minutes. I strolled through to the bathroom. Jensen hurriedly took my glass of Champagne and put it down. He pulled me towards him and kissed me gently on the lips, while his hands slowly undressed me. my clothes fell to the floor as he ran his hands over my naked body, lighting up every sense within me. My aroused nipples stood erect as his hands tweaked them, and a shiver ran down my spine. I began to undress Jensen, letting my hands glide over his muscled torso. He had a strong, firm body that reacted to my every touch. Jensen lifted me up and placed me into the bath which was full of bubbles, before climbing in beside me. We kissed and caressed as the bubbles encased our bodies, then we began to massage each other with the soapy lather. We spent ages, just touching and kissing each other. I didn't want to hurry into full sex, I wanted to savour every moment of the closeness that we were feeling. We must have spent at least an hour in the bath, as the water was cold when we emerged, and made our way to the bedroom, where we towel dried each other. We climbed into bed and held each other close, gently kissing. I wanted this moment to last forever. I wanted to savour each and every moment of our first night together as Mr and Mrs! I loved being with Jensen, he made me feel complete. I loved making love with him, but tonight I didn't want to hurry our lovemaking, I wanted to make it last forever. We lay in each other's arms, kissing and holding each other close until sunrise the following morning.

It had been a magical evening. We hadn't actually made love, but that was all about to change, as Jensen climbed on top of me and started to kiss every part of my body. His hands explored every inch of me and I began to moan with excitement as my body responded to his touch. Before long we were making love. Jensen's lovemaking was rhythmical and slow, but deep, and my body ached as I longed for him to climax into me. I didn't have long to wait as Jensen cried out my name, as he filled me with his seed. My body ached and I needed to relieve the sexual tension within me. Jensen rolled off me and lay on his back on the bed, his manhood still semi-hard, so I took it upon myself to tease it back to life. I began to gently stroke him and cares his balls, and before long, I'd achieved the desired result. I straddled Jensen and slid his cock deep into me. I could feel every ridge of his penis, and the ridges turned me on even more as I rode Jensen until I orgasmed. Exhausted, I rolled onto the bed next to Jensen and snuggled him until we were both fast asleep. We must have been tired, as we didn't wake up until lunch-time the following day. We ordered room service for lunch, where we feasted on poached salmon and lemon syllabub. We spent the rest of the afternoon just relaxing and lazing about. We'd planned to go out and have dinner in a nearby restaurant, but neither of us could be bothered to get out of our bathrobes, so we ordered room service, then spent the whole evening in bed, devouring each other!

The next morning we checked out of the hotel and headed back home. My parents were due to leave so they could catch their flight back to England. We had arranged for Tony and Sally to come over, and have a barbecue with my mum and dad, before they set off for the airport. We'd a lot to organise, so we wanted to get an early start. Once at home, my mother helped me prepare the food for the barbecue, and at 11 O'clock Tony and Sally arrived. Jensen got the barbecue going and we all enjoyed our lunch together. I was pleased that we all got on as a family, it was important to me that I bonded with Jensen's parents.

We all waved goodbye to my parents, as they had to leave to take the hire car back, before boarding their plane back to England. I didn't know when I would see them again, but Jensen told them that they were welcome to come and visit us in our home anytime, and unlike some folk, he meant it, and wasn't just being polite. Jensen only took a few more days off work, then embarked on his new business venture. He was excited and full of enthusiasm as he began organising some advertising. He did a leaflet drop in the surrounding towns, and it wasn't long before he received enquiries from customers, and the work began to come in. Jensen beamed with pride every time someone visited his new workshop. He had been hard at work, making new furniture to fill his showroom with. The barn had really taken shape, and Jensen had turned an empty barn into an amazingly successful business in a very short space of time. within a few weeks Jensen had secured a contract to supply a new hotel with furniture. The hotel proprietors were so impressed with the quality of his workmanship that they promised him another contract, to supply a further two of their hotels, in other countries, with new furniture. Jensen's business was going from strength to strength and he deserved it, he'd put so many hours into it. I knew he was feeling tired but he never once complained.

We hadn't been doing a lot of socialising over the last couple of months, as Jensen had been putting in twelve hour days in his workshop, and was too tired to think of going out. I didn't mind though, I know it sounds selfish, but I loved the fact that it was just the two of us. We planned to invite Jake, Melissa, Heather and Toby over to ours at the weekend. It was going to be a sort of celebration, as Jake and Melissa had just announced that they were going to get married. The weekend arrived, we all had an enjoyable evening. The wine was flowing and the conversation was buzzing. It had been a nice change, meeting up with friends and taking time off, to interact with other people. Jensen and I had been married for three months and we'd recently been talking a lot about babies. Jensen asked me if I wanted to have another baby. My initial reaction was that I wasn't sure. In a way I felt that, if I had another child, then it would be as if I'd forgotten about Chloe, which I would never do. Chloe would always have a place in my heart. I would spend hours in her memorial garden, talking away to her, hoping that she could hear me, up in heaven. But after I had given it some serious thought, I decided that I would like to try for another baby.

Jensen was so caring and told me that, should I feel that I couldn't go through with having another baby, then he would understand. That was so typical of Jensen, to be so understanding. His kindness and caring manner had been the decider for me to go ahead and try for another baby. I knew Jensen would be a good father, he wouldn't let life and work get in his way of his role as father, as Sebastian had done with Chloe. We agreed not to tell anyone about our plans to start a family, until I'd fallen pregnant. I didn't want to jinx us having a baby together. It was hard for me not to look through baby magazines and to speculate what colour to do the baby's room, but I didn't want to, in case I was unable to fall pregnant. After all, I was in my forties and the experts say that, the longer you leave it then the harder it can be to get pregnant. After a couple of months, and a missed period, the good news came, I was pregnant, Jensen and I were going to be parents! We telephoned everyone we knew, to tell them our good news. Both sets of parents were over the moon at the prospect of becoming grandparents, and our friends thought that it was about time. on hearing our good news, Heather organised a baby shower for the following week. I wasn't sure what a baby shower was. We didn't have them in England. Heather assured me that it was all the rage in America, and explained that it was just a few close friends and family who got together, brought gifts, and celebrated the new life that had just been created. 'Everything will be fine, just leave it to me!' She said.

On the day of the baby shower all our friends turned up. Sally came over to join the fun too, but unfortunately Tony and my parents weren't able to make it. Mum and dad were coming over a few weeks before I was due, to help out, and planned to stay for a month. Jensen had been busy building an extension to the house since hearing the news of his impending fatherhood, and it was nearly finished. All he needed to do was get someone in to wire up the electrics, so that he could finish off plastering the walls and carrying out the finishing touches. Jensen had created two extra bedrooms and an extra bathroom by building the extension. We'd already picked out a new bathroom suite which Jensen had installed, and it was waiting for its first use.

We had decided not to know the sex of our baby, it was to be a surprise, so we decided that we'd decorate the baby's bedroom in neutral colours. Thankfully all the work on the extension was to be completed in a week's time, which meant that we'd be able to start decorating and furnishing the room. Jensen had hand carved a cot for our new baby, it was the most beautiful item of furniture that I'd ever seen, much better than anything you could buy in the shops! Jensen had put his heart and soul into his masterpiece and I was so proud of him. We'd spent the last few weeks deciding on names and finally chose Jensen Junior if the baby was a boy, I liked the idea of naming a boy after his father. If our baby was a girl we were going to call her Lily.

A few days later and the extension was finally finished and we set about decorating it. We painted the walls of the baby's room taupe, having initially experimented with a lemon yellow colour which was way too bright! That was when we realised that the use of a soothing, restful colour would be better, and chose taupe, a nice calming colour and not so migraine inducing as the lemon yellow! We treated the spare bedroom to cornflower blue, which looked good against the white bedroom furniture, and made the room feel very clean and fresh. We decided that we'd use that room as a guest bedroom, for the times when our parents came to stay, or for times when our friends came over.

I had one month of my pregnancy left to go. Each night Jensen would fall asleep on my stomach, whilst listening to our baby moving around inside me. I didn't think that I'd go full term, I could tell that our baby was getting restless, as I hadn't had a good night's sleep in weeks. My overnight bag was packed and ready, and on permanent standby. What a state I was in. I was heavily pregnant, I felt fat and frumpy, and to top it all off, tomorrow was my birthday! I would be forty-three. I was in no mood to celebrate, especially as my feet kept swelling up like balloons. I'd been to the doctor about it, and had been advised to rest as much as possible. I took the doctor's advice very seriously, after all I didn't want to take any risks. Getting pre-eclampsia was something I wanted to avoid at all costs!

Jensen decided that it would be best if we stayed in, to minimise any risk, and had planned to make me a special meal. The next morning I woke to Jensen bringing me breakfast in bed. There were lots of cards and presents for me to open, from all of our family and friends. Jensen had bought me a gold necklace, in the shape of a rainbow, my parents had sent me over some money, and sally had given me a painting, of Jensen and I standing underneath the arbour on our wedding day. Sally had enclosed a letter saying that she had copied the painting from a photograph that she'd taken at our wedding. Tony had sent over a bottle of my favourite perfume, and Jake, Melissa, Heather and Toby had clubbed together to get me a day pass for the health spa nearby, which I could use after the baby was born.

I was waited on, hand and foot by Jensen for the rest of the day, and while I took a shower he prepared our meal. I made an effort to get dressed up, it was the least I could do. I'd put on quite a bit of weight throughout my pregnancy, and I was a bit limited for clothing choice. I didn't want to wear pregnancy clothes, they all looked like oversized, floral tents! I'd just gone out and bought bigger sized, normal, every-day clothes instead. I finally decided to wear my navy dress, it was simple, but comfortable. I put my hair up in a clip and put on my make-up. Jensen called out to let me know that dinner was ready to be served.

He'd cooked a lasagne, served with salad, and pudding was a chocolate cake. Jensen remarked, over dinner, how beautiful I was. my hair had grown longer, and although I'd put it up in a clip, it seemed to fall round my face in curls. We enjoyed a lovely night and I went to bed feeling like a princess!

The weeks flew by, and Jensen was getting busier and busier at work, so busy in fact, that he'd taken on two staff to help with the workload, and Tony and my parents had flown in from England. Sally had been a big help, coming over every couple of days, to see if I needed anything doing. Jake and Melissa's wedding was now only a week away, and I was due in ten days time. I'd had a few false alarms, times when I thought I'd gone into labour. They were usually during the night and not ideal! Jake and Melissa were getting married at the local church, and were being married by the same Reverend that had married Jensen and I. I wanted to help out with their wedding, so I made lots of little bags of favours, one for each guest. I made them out of voile, and put sugared almonds in them, topping off each bag with ribbon that matched the colour of her bridesmaids dresses. Their reception was to be a sit down meal, and was being held at the restaurant where Jensen had proposed to me!

It was Jake and Melissa's wedding day. I wasn't feeling at my best, as I'd been up all night with backache. I jumped in the shower to try and wake myself up a little, before putting on the new dress I'd bought for this special occasion, and Jensen put on his best suit.

My parents had been invited to the wedding too, so my mother was trying to get ready, in between helping my dad with his tie and shoes! My dad had bought some new leather shoes and was complaining that they were too tight. My mother was running about, filling each shoe with newspaper, and telling my dad it was meant to stretch them!

My back pains were getting stronger by the hour and I had an awful feeling that today would be the day our baby would make its entrance! I just hoped that I could hang on until after the wedding! I didn't tell anyone that my back pain was getting worse, everybody would have panicked and insisted that I stayed at home. No way would I miss Jake and Melissa's wedding, I wasn't going to do that. I was confident that I could get through the wedding service without going into full blown labour. We set off for the church, and on arrival, took our seats. Jake stood at the front, with Toby, his best man, by his side. Jake had originally asked Jensen to be his best man, but with me being as far on in my pregnancy as I was, Jensen had asked Jake if he would mind if he said 'No', as he didn't want to let Jake down. He would need to dash off if I went into labour, and that wouldn't be fair, Jake was very understanding. Melissa looked beautiful as she walked down the aisle. She and Jake had been seeing each other for two years. They were meant to be together, they seemed to fit hand in glove, and they were very close, just as Jensen and I were. I felt this would also be a marriage that would stand the test of time!

I'd managed to keep my back pain under some sort of control, but I was beginning to wonder how much longer I could go on, before telling Jensen. At the reception, during the speeches, I had to give in and tell Jensen that I was in labour. My contractions were coming every ten minutes, and I needed to get to the hospital. We let Jake and Melissa know our plans, thanked them for a wonderful day, then left to drive to the hospital which was about ten minutes drive from our house. We had to pass our house to get to the hospital, so we made a stop to pick up my overnight case. Within minutes of our arrival at hospital I was ushered into the delivery suite just in time, as ten minutes later, our son Jensen Junior was born. He weighed in at eight pounds, had blonde hair like his dad, and his eyes were blue-green, he was perfect!

Jensen rang everyone to tell them that he had a son, in fact, my parents were still at the wedding reception when Jake announced our good news over the microphone! I was so happy, tired, but happy. Jensen stood next to me, holding my hand as I gave birth to our son. He was fabulous, he wept as the doctor handed his son to him. By the look on Jensen's face I could tell that they'd immediately bonded. As I'd given birth before, I didn't need to stay in hospital overnight and went home five hours later, having caught up on some sleep. All our parents were waiting at the house for us when we returned home, eagerly waiting to meet their new grandchild. Jensen Junior was introduced to the family and was an instant hit. He was sure to be spoilt rotten by both sets of grandparents, he would want for nothing and love would be in constant supply. Over the following few months, we settled into a new routine. Jensen as expected, was a great dad. He got up for the four-hourly feeds and nappy changes, he was a natural! He was a doting dad and I was pleased. I knew that our child was to be brought up in a close, happy, loving household.

My parents had gone home armed with loads of photo's of our new arrival, to show their friends and neighbours. Tony had also returned to England, to sell his house! He and Sally were going to give their relationship another go. I knew they'd become closer since our wedding, and Jensen was delighted at the prospect of his mum and dad reuniting. Heather had married her boyfriend of six months, whilst Toby declared he was going to stay single. Jake and Melissa had some good news of their own, they too were expecting, Melissa had conceived on their wedding night!

And if you're wondering what happened to Sebastian and Charlotte, well, wonder no longer. Charlotte moved back to England whilst Jensen and I were holidaying in the Maldives. She moved in with Sebastian straight away, married two months later, and after three months of marriage she left him! She'd been seeing someone in her new place of work, and declared that she was in love. She divorced Sebastian and took half of his wealth. Unfortunately, her new man turned out to be a conman, had ripped her off and squandered all her divorce settlement. She was, apparently, now living in a bed-sit, had been fired from her job when the bosses wife had found out that she'd seduced her husband at an office party. Sebastian had to sell the house that we'd had together, just to pay Charlotte off. He is, by all accounts, living in a one-bedroom flat in London now. So all in all, I think everyone got just what they deserved. What's that saying. Revenge is a dish best served cold! Well Sebastian certainly got his comeuppance. He'd lost everything that had been important to him, money and control! I don't see Charlotte ever settling down. She'll continue to go from relationship to relationship, regardless of whether they are married or not. She seems unable to settle with just one person, chasing the idea that she deserves better. I've no doubt she'll manage to escape her current situation, and life in a bed-sit, after all, there will always be other men eager to meet her acquaintance and give everything up for her. Jensen has just expanded her business and has had to build another barn, just to be able to keep up with demand for his furniture. My parents are currently toying with the idea of moving over here to be closer to us. They're now in their seventies and are worried that before long, they'll be too old or too infirm to travel over to see us all. They miss Jensen Junior like crazy. Jensen and I have discussed having another baby, but we'll have to wait and see. I want to enjoy Jensen Junior as long as possible before getting pregnant again. We've talked about moving to a bigger house, but neither Jensen or I can bear to leave this house, besides, Chloe's memorial garden is here and I wouldn't want to dig it up and re-place it somewhere else. I feel at peace in this house, I did from the very first moment I visited it, and to top it off I often see

Chloe's rainbows in the sky. Jensen and I have just celebrated the second anniversary of our first meeting, and we've been married nearly a year-and-a-half now. So, all in all, my life couldn't get any better. I am fulfilled, and the emptiness that I once felt inside has gone. For the first time in my life, I am complete!

I trust you've enjoyed taking every step of my journey with me, sharing the laughter and the pain along the way. Just remember that no matter what life throws at you, you can get through it. I didn't think I would ever have a loving relationship after finding out about Sebastian's affair, or indeed, have another child after losing Chloe. But fate looked kindly on me and gave me a reason to live and taught me to appreciate everything I have. Meeting Jensen has been my saving grace, and for that I thank him. Just remember, when times get tough and you feel lost, somewhere out there, is someone like Jensen, someone to make your life better, someone to make you complete! Life is for living, so go ahead and grab every opportunity that you can, and be happy.

The End.

Lightning Source UK Ltd.
Milton Keynes UK
UKOW04f0343070214

226048UK00001B/3/P